The Instant Guide to Healthy

Cacti

Series editor: David Longman

Colour illustrations by Josephine Martin

The Instant Guide to Healthy

Cacti

*John
Pilbeam*

Times
BOOKS

THE AUTHOR

John Pilbeam has grown, studied and written about cacti for over thirty years. He is Secretary of The Mammillaria Society, a qualified judge of the British National Cactus and Succulent Society and a member of the International Organization for Succulent Plant Study.

Originally published in Great Britain in 1984 as *How to Care for Your Cacti* by Peter Lowe, London.

Library of Congress Catalog Card Number: 84-40639
International Standard Book Number: 0-8129-1179-2

Printed in Italy by Amilcare Pizzi SpA

9 8 7 6 5 4 3 2 1
First American Edition

Contents

Introduction

Cacti are among the most fascinating houseplants and many enthusiasts grow them to the exclusion of all others. They are also among the most undemanding of plants and, perhaps because of this, are often not grown to their full potential. Though they do not need much attention, it is important to provide the correct care and conditions and to understand why these are necessary. Only then will they grow well.

The main part of this book shows the principal genera of cacti worth cultivating in the home and gives details of the care and conditions each one requires for best possible results. Each 2-page spread covers one genus. A colour painting shows the most attractive or easily available cactus in the genus and there are photos of other species and line drawings to illustrate care details. Some genera have only one or two species of interest, others have a hundred or more. All have their individual beauty to be discovered and appreciated.

The introduction gives general instructions for cultivation with useful step-by-step illustrations and includes an important section which enables you to identify at a glance what may go wrong with your plants. Here colour paintings show the problems caused by pests, diseases, neglect – or too much attention of the wrong kind – and captions explain how to deal with them. Most problems are common to all cacti and the symptoms look similar from plant to plant. Check plants regularly and use these pages as reference when ever your plant shows signs of ill health.

Light and temperature

The most important factor in caring for cacti is light. Their healthy growth, the amount of spines and number of flowers produced are directly related to the amount of light you allow them. Ideally the all-round light of a sun-bathed greenhouse is what they need, but an uncurtained sunny windowsill will do very well for most cacti. In winter months,

Tools for cactus gardening.
Cacti can be cared for with very little special equipment and you can acquire what you need gradually as your collection grows.

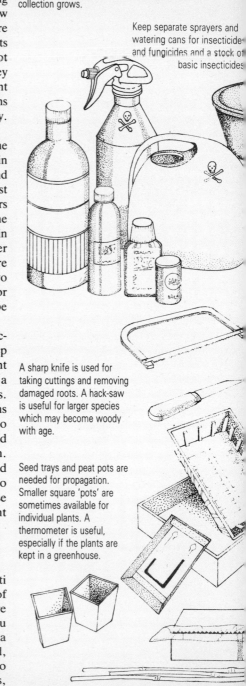

Keep separate sprayers and watering cans for insecticide and fungicides and a stock of basic insecticides

A sharp knife is used for taking cuttings and removing damaged roots. A hack-saw is useful for larger species which may become woody with age.

Seed trays and peat pots are needed for propagation. Smaller square 'pots' are sometimes available for individual plants. A thermometer is useful, especially if the plants are kept in a greenhouse.

6

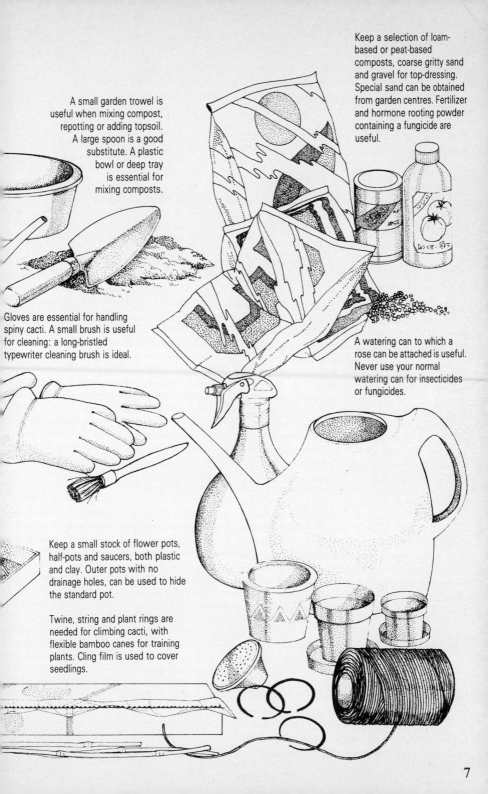

A small garden trowel is useful when mixing compost, repotting or adding topsoil. A large spoon is a good substitute. A plastic bowl or deep tray is essential for mixing composts.

Keep a selection of loam-based or peat-based composts, coarse gritty sand and gravel for top-dressing. Special sand can be obtained from garden centres. Fertilizer and hormone rooting powder containing a fungicide are useful.

Gloves are essential for handling spiny cacti. A small brush is useful for cleaning: a long-bristled typewriter cleaning brush is ideal.

A watering can to which a rose can be attached is useful. Never use your normal watering can for insecticides or fungicides.

Keep a small stock of flower pots, half-pots and saucers, both plastic and clay. Outer pots with no drainage holes, can be used to hide the standard pot.

Twine, string and plant rings are needed for climbing cacti, with flexible bamboo canes for training plants. Cling film is used to cover seedlings.

when light levels are lower, it is more important still to ensure that they remain in the lightest positions possible. If indoors keep them on the windowsill, only removing them at night if you close the curtains, otherwise in cold climates they may be damaged in the ice-box created between the curtains and the glass on frosty nights. If in a greenhouse, a minimum winter temperature of 40°F (5°C), or better 45°F (7°C), should be maintained.

If a greenhouse is very exposed to summer sunshine, it may be necessary to shade the glass at times to prevent scorching. Cacti seem particularly vulnerable to this in the spring, when the sun suddenly shines strongly after weeks of cloudy weather and the cacti are a little on the soft side, especially if they have recently been watered and have swelled up after their winter rest. Good air circulation will also prevent scorching, and some growers remove end panes of glass to improve the air flow. Try to keep the greenhouse temperature below 100°F (38°C).

Watering

In the wild cacti receive water at certain times of the year only, and then often in quantity, with flash floods washing over or submerging them for hours at a time. However, the water drains away quickly and the plants must be able to take it up rapidly and store it for long periods of drought. This is made possible by their concertina-like tissues which swell or contract to a remarkable degree, and the thick, often waxy exterior surface, which minimizes water loss through evaporation.

For best results indoors, try to imitate natural conditions as closely as possible. In the growing period, from spring until early autumn, water as for most other plants, but start slowly in the spring after the dry winter spell, leaving long gaps between watering so that the soil dries out almost completely each time. By early summer, when the sun is strong, the plants can be watered every week, provided still that they are almost dry

from the previous watering. Never leave cacti standing in a saucer of water. A plant label or knife blade will quickly show if the soil is still moist: if it comes out from being stuck into the compost clean, the soil is dry; if it comes out smeared with moist soil, leave it for a few days before giving more water. In the autumn the gaps between waterings should become longer, until by mid-autumn for plants in 5in (13cm) or larger pots, and early winter for those in smaller pots, watering should cease until the spring. Some growers believe in not allowing the soil to dry out completely, and give a little throughout the winter. This is all right if minimum temperatures of about 50°F (10°C) are maintained, but there is a danger of encouraging lanky, uncharacteristic growth, of discouraging the formation of flower-buds, or even of losing the plants altogether. It is safer to leave them dry.

Feeding

Cacti need a fertilizer based on a high potash content, like those for tomatoes, roses or chrysanthemums. Probably the easiest to use are those in liquid form. Use them at the strength recommended for use on potted plants. Regular feeding ensures strong growth of both the stems and the spines and increases the chances of flowers being produced. Some species need more feeding than others, and the individual entries give their requirements. Always dilute the fertilizer as instructed or the plant's roots may be burned.

Some fertilizers leave unsightly stains on plants if they are poured over the top of them, so that it is best to water around them instead. Wiping gently with a damp brush will remove stains if they are made.

Soil

Cacti need a well-drained, nutritious mixture, which will allow good root development and supply water but will not stay soggy for too long at a time. Either loam-based or peat-based composts can be used

Repotting

1–2 weeks before repotting, water soil so that root ball will come from the pot easily.

4. Trickle fresh compost around root ball, firming it down gently around base of plant.

1. Hold plant gently round base of stem, with gloves on if plant is spiny. Tap pot rim against edge of table or bench and gently ease root ball out onto a clear space. Check roots for root mealy bug and growth.

2. If root ball is compact with plenty of roots and no mealy bug, do not disturb it but prepare new pot one size larger with layer of compost deep enough to plant the root ball at the same level as before, about 1in (2½cm) below rim of pot. Place root ball on new compost.

3. If compost falls away easily but there is a good root system or if plant has reached its maximum size, carefully shake off old soil from around roots.

5. Add a final layer of grit to top of compost. Do not water for 2 weeks after repotting.

s a basis. Do not use unsterile garden soil.

Loam-based compost is made up of terilized loam (soil) mixed with peat and grit or coarse, washed sand. It is usually sold with fertilizer added, following formulae developed by the John Innes Institute for Horticultural Research. The numbers 1, 2 and 3 indicate the different proportions of fertilizer added with 1 the weakest and 3 the richest mixture. In this book they are referred to as 'loam-based Nos. 1, 2 or 3.'

Either loam-based or peat-based composts can be used neat, but to encourage more rapid drying out, they are best mixed with 1 part of coarse, gritty sand to 2 parts of compost. On no account use builders' or seashore sand which will not be sterile and may have a high lime or salt content. The amount of sand can be varied according to the needs of particular plants, and this is specified in the individual entries. Special cactus composts are available but are often worse than a good home-made mixture.

Repotting

Plastic pots have almost entirely superseded clay ones for cactus cultivation, although for some plants, such as *Ariocarpus*, which come from very arid areas, clay has advantages: it allows moisture to evaporate very quickly so that the compost is never moist for more than a few days at a time. For these more difficult cacti, increasing the grit content of the compost up to 60 or even 70% enables you to achieve similar conditions with plastic pots.

Many cacti are shallow-rooted and will do better in half-pots or pans shallower than their width. Those with thick, tuberous roots need sufficient depth to contain the roots without cramping them.

If you have a greenhouse collection of cacti, consider using square rather than round pots. These make the maximum use of space, provide more root room, and fit together so as to hide each other from view.

The best time for repotting is in late winter to early spring, before fresh roots have started to develop. Check the condition of the plant's roots when you have removed it from its pot. If the root ball is solid and there are plenty of new roots, repot it in a pot one size larger than the old one. If the compost falls away easily but there is a good root system, the plant can be repotted in the same sized pot with fresh compost. This also applies to plants that are nearly full-grown and are in pots 5in (13cm) or more. If using the same pot, wash it out well before replanting.

Always plant the cactus at the same level

Growing from seed

1. Prepare 3½in (9cm) half pots or seed trays with soil-less or good loam based No.1 potting compost and a layer of fine grit on the surface.

2. Sow seed thinly on the surface and do not cover with compost.

3. Water from below with fungicide diluted to strength recommended for damping off of seedlings until surface looks moist.

4. Cover pots or tray with polythene, sealing ends and sides to prevent moisture from escaping.

5. Keep at 70°F (21°C) in light place, not direct sunlight, for 6 months or more, until seedlings are the size of a small garden pea. Do not water unless moisture film on polythene becomes patchy or dries out.

6. Prick out seedlings into new trays or small pots, planting about 1in (2½cm) apart.

Cuttings

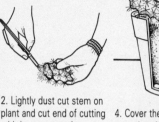

1. Cut stem with a sharp knife at the narrowest possible point. Cut at a slight angle.

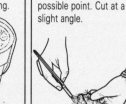

2. Lightly dust cut stem on plant and cut end of cutting with hormone rooting powder containing fungicide and leave cutting to dry for 2 days.

3. When cut surface is thoroughly dry, prepare small pot with dry compost and place cutting on surface.

4. Cover the cut end just enough to hold it upright or lean it against the side of the pot.

5. Water after about 2–4 weeks when roots have started to grow from base. This encourages roots to penetrate compost.

---

as it was before and add a final top layer of washed grit to the compost. This prevents the compost becoming compacted into a hard layer after watering, stops it splashing up around the plant and marking the lower spines and helps to prevent too rapid drying out in hot weather.

Propagation

For some cacti propagation is so easy that they need little assistance from the grower. For others it is so difficult that for the amateur even to try is a waste of time. Fortunately most cacti fall in the middle of these two extremes and with a little care can be propagated from either cuttings or from seed.

Seeds: In the wild cactus seedlings survive only in sheltered, damp places: they are at first so tiny that they need protection from the scorching sun. Imitate their natural habitats with an atmosphere enclosed by polythene or cling film. The best time to sow the seed is in spring, provided that a steady temperature of 70°F (21°C) can be given until the seeds have germinated. A layer of fine grit added to the surface of the compost will help to combat algae which will smother the seedlings if they get a hold.

Cuttings: The basic method of taking cuttings is illustrated on p. 10. Remember that unlike any other sort of plant, cacti must never be placed straight into fresh compost and watered. The cut surface must be allowed to harden or harmful fungi may invade the tissue. Do not water them until small new roots have started to appear.

Grafting: Certain cacti are difficult to grow on their own roots and some variegated types cannot survive at all on their own roots indoors. These plants are usually grafted onto a rootstock which is easier to grow (see p.26.) Unlike cuttings, the cut ends must not be allowed to dry out at all but must be pressed together immediately. The most important thing is to ensure that the rings near the centre of the stem (the vascular bundles) overlap. If the graft is successful, the upper plant should show growth after about 3 months, as it takes on the vigour of the rootstock. Remember to provide conditions that are right for the rootstock, especially if it is more demanding than the plant grafted on to it.

Pests and insecticides

When pests attack they are very difficult to eradicate completely and the damage they can cause may be irreparable.

To prevent attacks, spray regularly with insecticides, once a month in the growing season and once or twice when the cacti are dormant in winter. In the growing period use both contact and systemic insecticides. Contact insecticides are sprayed and kill when they contact the pest; systemics are either sprayed or watered into the soil. They work both by contact and by entering the plant's system so that any sap-sucking insect takes in the poison as it feeds. In winter use only contact sprays, in dry weather, so that the plant does not stay wet for too long.

Insecticides are dangerous to humans and animals as well as to pests. Spray plants outside in the early morning on a fine, still day, out of direct sunlight. Leave them out for several hours. In a greenhouse, work from the far end towards the door. Keep out until the vapour has dispersed.

Taking care with insecticides

Insecticides and fungicides may contain deadly chemicals. Use them with care.

Never mix different types of insecticides as the chemicals may react.
Never put them into other bottles, such as soft drink or beer bottles.
Never breathe in the spray.
Never spray in windy weather.
Never pour them down the sink or drains. Do not even pour the water in which you have washed containers and sprayers down the drain.
Never make up more at one time than you will use.
Never keep diluted insecticide for more than 24 hours.
Never leave old containers lying around.
Never stay in a greenhouse after spraying.

Always follow instructions carefully. Do not over or under dilute.
Always use a separate watering can and sprayer, keeping another one for normal spraying and watering.
Always keep away from food, crockery, glasses, food containers, and minerals. Derris is harmful to fish; malathion harms bees.
Always cover fish bowls when spraying.
Always store them with their sprayers and containers in a dry, frost free place, on a high shelf out of reach of children.
Always spray outside, when bees are not around. Early morning best.
Always wash out all sprayers and empty bottles after use, inside and out.
Always pour washing water onto ground away from food crops and water sources such as streams and rivers.
Always throw empty bottles and containers away with domestic waste.
Always wash thoroughly in hot water and detergent when you have used them.

If you inspect your cacti regularly and act quickly at the first sign of trouble, most conditions can be successfully treated. The pictures on the following pages show what to look out for; the captions explain what is causing the problem and how to put it right.

Brown marks appear on plant's skin, especially after winter. Brown spots and blotches appear on skin.

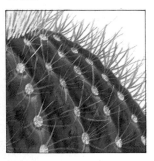

Skin turns light brown. Fine webs between spines and, under magnifying glass, tiny red brown mites moving about.

Patches that look like cotton wool on skin, especially near growing point or around base

Cold marks caused by keeping plant in too low a temperature in winter.

Do not cut marks out. They are unsightly but not fatal. Check plant's temperature requirements. If on a windowsill in the home, do not leave between curtain and glass in winter.

Red spider mite.

Spray with contact insecticide to kill pests and/or systemic insecticide to protect the plant from further attack. Check that both types of insecticide specify red spider. Repeat every 2 weeks for next 3 months, then treat regularly 2 to 3 times a year as a preventative measure. Keep newly purchased plants separate until you are sure they are pest free or other plants will quickly be infected.

Mealy bug, small woodlouse-like creature about 1/8in (2–3mm) long, covered with white, flour-like coating. They surround themselves with the wool in which to lay eggs.

Remove bugs and wool with small paintbrush or cotton bud dipped in methylated spirits. This immobilizes pest but may not kill it. Use a toothpick or broken matchstick to reach between the spines. Then spray with diluted malathion or other contact insecticide or, especially for woolly plants, water systemic insecticide into soil. Repeat after 10 days.

what goes wrong

Growing point whitish or yellowish grey, plant becoming elongated with much narrower new growth than old. A plant normally free standing may need support to keep it upright.

Skin wrinkles, shrinks and looks dull.

Plant skin looks brown or black and is soft to the touch. Plant does not grow. No small flies around plant.

Lack of light. Plant is reaching towards best light and so growing unnaturally.

Put into better all round light position, on a sunny windowsill. For first two weeks shade with white paper to accustom plant gradually to strong sunlight. Always keep in best possible light in winter or flower buds may not form and plant will not flower the following year.

If during dry period in winter, natural contraction. If in growing season, too dry or, if watering correct, root loss or too much sudden sunshine.

In winter leave dry but spray overhead on sunny mornings. At other times of the year, check conditions. Water if dried out and if in strong sunlight, shade with white paper at hottest times of the year. If roots rotted, may be overwatering (see p. 14).

Plant is dead, usually from overwatering, watering in cold months or frosting.

Remove plant from others and dispose of plant and soil. Wash pot thoroughly before re-use and do not use soil for other plants. Be more careful to allow plants to dry out between waterings, keep dry in winter and for 2 weeks after repotting or root disturbance. Protect from low·temperatures and do not trap plants between curtains and glass indoors on cold nights.

13

Small round brown patches with raised centre, like miniature limpets, on stems.

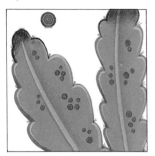

Plant does not grow but feels firm to the touch and is not surrounded by tiny black flies. On removing from pot, no roots visible. Possibly brown or orange patches on base.

Small green insects cluster around buds and soft growing points, leaving sticky substance.

Roots have rotted through, usually from overwatering or stale, compacted compost.

Brush away soil from base of plant and leave to dry for 2 days. Then with a sharp knife pare away thin layers from base of plant until no brown or orange patches remain. Dust base with hormone rooting powder containing fungicide, brush off surplus and leave plant out of its pot to dry for a week (more if the cut area is more than 1in, 3cm wide). Prepare new pot with fresh compost and place plant on top. Do not water until roots appear. Then treat normally, taking care with watering.

Scale insect. Tiny insect is inside waxy scale, sucking plant's sap.

Spray with contact insecticide or water soil with systemic insecticide and, after a few days, pick off scales with tweezers or thumb nail. Scale insect is unsightly but not usually fatal. As for other pests, keep infected plant isolated and examine newly bought plants carefully before putting them with others.

Greenfly.

Spray with insecticide or derris, repeating every week until clear. Keep away from other plants. Sticky substance may cause mould if not treated. Derris, a plant-based product, is safest treatment especially in the house.

14

Plant does not grow when repotted, cotton wool-like patches found on roots, with tiny white sausage-shaped bugs about ⅛in (1-2mm) long.

Root mealy bug.

Wash soil off roots thoroughly to remove all traces of pest. Agitate washed roots in solution of contact insecticide. Allow to dry completely (2–3 days) before repotting in clean pot with fresh soil. Throw away old soil and scrub old pot before using again. If repotting in the growing season, do not water for at least 2 weeks or if in the winter months, not until spring. Other plants may be infected. If no obvious signs, place plants in their pots in bowl and soak them for half an hour in a solution of contact insecticide. Liquid should be deep enough to cover soil.

Brown marks on side of plant facing the light.

Plant is scorched. Soft growth made while out of direct sunlight will burn if suddenly exposed to sunshine.

Cacti are especially vulnerable in spring after the dry winter period if sun suddenly shines strongly. Accustom them to stronger light gradually by shading with white paper or moving into lighter area by degrees. Damage is irreparable, but plants will usually recover and grow on unless growing point is burned.

Plant does not grow and tiny black flies are around base of plant.

Plant attacked by sciara fly larvae, feeding on roots and plant tissue.

Examine roots for damage and cut back to healthy tissue. Spray plant with insecticide to kill flies and stand pot in bowl filled with solution of contact or systemic insecticide to kill larvae. Liquid should cover soil. Leave until soil thoroughly wet (½ an hour) then drain and allow to dry out. Repeat every two months or whenever flies appear.

Acanthocalycium

A small genus of cacti from northern Argentina, there are 4 or 5 different species of Acanthocalycium available. They are mostly very spiny plants, with densely spiny flower-buds, too, which look like thistle buds as they emerge. They make single, unclustering, globular plants (although offsets are sometimes produced after about 5 years), up to about 5–6in (12–15cm) wide. They have black, brown or grey spines arranged on vertical ribs on a dark green stem. *Acanthocalycium violaceum* (p.17) has lilac-coloured flowers (unusual for a cactus) but other species have white, pink, orange-red or yellow flowers. They flower when about 3in (7–8cm) wide, at about 4 years, and rarely need more than a 5in (13cm) pot unless they are kept for 8–10 years when they may outgrow it.

Acanthocalycium brevispinum is less common than *A.violaceum*. Its spines are shorter and more rigid and its yellow flowers grow from the side. Like the other species, it must be allowed to dry out almost completely between watering and kept quite dry if the temperature falls to around 40°F (4°C).

Light: Maximum sunshine is needed for flower production, and to ensure good strong spines. Ideally grow outside in the summer months, bringing them gradually into full sun if they have not had much in winter. If grown in a greenhouse they will not need shading.

Temperature: Not less than 40°F (4°C); keep below 100°F (38°C) and give fresh air in summer months.

Water: Water well (overhead except when flowering), about once a fortnight in the summer months, or more frequently for smaller pots (3in, 8cm or less), making sure they have almost dried out from the previous watering before doing so. Keep dry in the 3 coldest months except for an overhead spray every 8 weeks.

Feeding: Once a month in spring and summer with a high potash fertilizer (as used for tomatoes).

Soil: Use 2 parts of either soil-less compost or loam-based No. 2 potting compost with 1 part coarse gritty sand (not builders' or seashore).

Repotting: Repot annually in the spring into next size pot, until a 5in (13cm) pot is reached, when every other year will do, unless the plant is outgrowing the pot it is in.

Cleaning and pest control: Spray overhead with a forceful spray of water if plant gets dusty and include an insecticide about 3 times a year.

Other species: Some of the rarer species are worth seeking out: *A. brevispinum* or *A. thionanthum* with deep yellow flowers and short, rigid spines like carpet tacks; *A. spiniflorum*, with pink flowers; *A. Klimpelianum*, with pure white flowers; *A. peitscheranum*, with white flowers delicately flushed pink; and the variably coloured flowers of *A. variiflorum*, which range from yellow to orange-red or carmine in colour.

Growing from seed

1. In spring, prepare seed tray or 2in (5cm) pots with soil-less seedling or good loam-based seed or No. 1 potting compost. Add layer of fine grit to surface, leaving ½in (1cm) space between surface and rim.

2. Sow seed thinly on surface and tap sides of pot/tray to settle seed in the grit. Then water from base with fungicide diluted to strength for 'damping off' of seedlings, until surface is damp.

3. Cover pots or tray with polythene, folding ends underneath or sealing with sticky tape to seal in moisture. Leave in light (not direct sunlight) at 70°F (21°C). Do not water again unless condensation on polythene becomes patchy or dries up.

4. After 6 months, or following spring for safety, prick out separately into 2in (5cm) pots or ½in (1cm) apart in seed trays.

These cacti need very good light all year round. If they are in too dark a position they will grow out of shape, the tip becoming elongated with the spines weaker at the top. Without full summer sun they are unlikely to flower and are best kept outside or in a greenhouse in summer.

Acanthocalycium violaceum has long, flexible, curving, yellowish-brown spines through which the pale lilac flowers push with difficulty at the top of the plant. A healthy plant will have fresh, brighter coloured spines appearing at the centre during spring and summer and should produce flowers after it is about 3in (7–8cm) wide. Each flower lasts about a week.

Aporocactus

There are some half-dozen species of this genus of hanging cactus, the commonest of which, *Aporocactus flagelliformis* (p.19), has been grown on windowsills for many years and is popularly known as the Rat's-tail cactus from the form of its limp, hanging stems. Other species have more rigidity but still make good plants for hanging baskets and are suitable for porches in the summer. They should never be left out in winter, however, for as natives of southern Mexico, they cannot stand low temperatures. *Aporocactus flagelliformis* produces flowers all along its stems in early spring. There are also some very attractive flowering hybrids, crosses between Aporocactus species and Epiphyllums (known as Aporophyllums) and other related large-flowered species. These make springy-stemmed, semi-pendant plants, also very suitable for hanging baskets, and usually flowering freely.

Aporophyllum 'Rosemary' is a hybrid produced by crossing an Aporocactus with an Epiphyllum. The inner petals are pink, the outer more salmon-coloured. Like true Aporocactus species, they are best kept in hanging baskets.

Light: Best on a sunny windowsill indoors, or hung from the upper part of the window-frame, so that their stems can hang in the light. If grown in a greenhouse, shade lightly in summer as strong sun through glass may scorch the stems.

Temperature: Not less than 40°F (4°C); keep below 100°F (38°C) and give fresh air in summer months.

Water: Water weekly in the spring and summer, so that soil just dries out between waterings and give just enough in the winter to stop them drying out completely. Once every 3–4 weeks is probably enough. Spray once a week in spring and summer and once every 6–8 weeks in winter.

Feeding: Once a month in spring and summer with a high potash fertilizer (as used for tomatoes).

Soil: Use soil-less compost with no grit.

Repotting: Repot each year in spring into next size pot until in 6in (15cm) pot or basket. After this, repot in same sized container each year with fresh compost, after shaking off as much of the old soil as possible. Leave dry after repotting for a fortnight. If becoming too large for container or available space, remove some of its stems and use as cuttings.

Cleaning and pest control: Spray with water weekly in spring and summer to keep the dust off and in winter spray about once every 6–8 weeks. Add insecticide to the spray 2 or 3 times a year.

Other species: Except A. *flagelliformis* few are seen: A. *flagriformis* and A. *conzatti* the most likely. These are, however, less interesting than the hybrids which have flowers ranging from pale pink to deepest red.

18

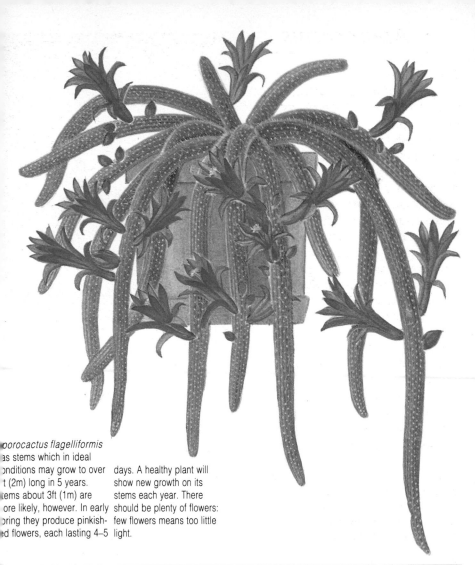

...porocactus flagelliformis ...as stems which in ideal ...onditions may grow to over ...t (2m) long in 5 years. ...tems about 3ft (1m) are ...ore likely, however. In early ...oring they produce pinkish- ...d flowers, each lasting 4–5 days. A healthy plant will show new growth on its stems each year. There should be plenty of flowers: few flowers means too little light.

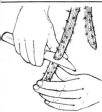

Taking cuttings
1. After flowering finished, cut lengths of stem 2–3in (5–8cm) long with sharp knife, cutting at an angle.

2. Dust end of cutting and cut end of stem with hormone rooting powder containing fungicide. Leave cutting to dry for at least 2 days.

3. Prepare 2 or 3in (5 or 8cm) pot with potting compost and place cutting on surface.

4. Cover just enough to hold it upright or rest tip against side of pot. Keep in light (not sunny) place for 2–3 weeks until roots develop. Then start watering. Repot when roots fill pot.

Ariocarpus

Sometimes known as Fossil cacti or 'Living rocks' these plants are the ancients of the Mexican deserts, growing so slowly and to such a great age that imported plants are often considerably older than their owners, sometimes a hundred years old or more. They were once usually seen as imported wild plants but more and more smaller, seedling plants are now being raised commercially as plants in the wild must be conserved and protected. In fact imported plants are difficult to establish and it is advisable to check that they show signs of new wool in the centre before buying them, unless you are experienced in inducing the wizened, turnip-like roots to send out fresh growth. Take care not to damage these larger roots and, if they are broken or bruised, dry them off and dust them liberally with rooting powder. Young seedling plants present fewer problems, except that they are so slow growing and may take 20 years to reach 6in (15cm) across. Grafting will help to increase the growth rate and this is best done at an early seedling stage.

Ariocarpus furfuraceus may grow as large as 7in (18cm) across and is made up of triangular tubercles like thick leaves, in a rosette three times as wide as it is tall. The large, white flower pushes up through a mass of fresh, yellow-brown wool at the centre of the plant; the appearance of new wool is a sure sign that this slow-growing plant is flourishing.

Ariocarpus kotschoubeyanus belongs to the smaller-growing group, rarely needing more than a 4in (10cm) pot. Its white or purple-pink flowers appear in late summer and autumn. Do not water until compost has dried out from previous watering — and keep dry in winter.

Light: Maximum light is essential. Keep on the sunniest windowsill or in an unshaded greenhouse.

Temperature: Not less than 40°F (4°C); keep below 100°F (38°C) and give fresh air in the summer months.

Water: Water well every 2 weeks in summer only. Keep dry in winter. Spraying is unnecessary.

Feeding: Not necessary, but will induce a little more growth; use high potash fertilizer, as for tomatoes.

Soil: A high grit content is advisable, with up to 75% coarse, gritty sand (not builders' r seashore) to 25% soil-less or good loam-based compost.

Repotting: Avoid disturbing roots too often once plant is established, for mature plants, 3–4in, 8–10cm across) repotting only every third year. Young plants may be repotted into next size pot in spring.

Cleaning and pest control: Spray lightly if dusty and gently brush up wool when dry. Add insecticide to the cleaning spray 3 or 4 times a year.

Other species: There are two main groups, the first including *A. lloydii* (below), growing up to about 7in (18cm) across. Of the other large species the best are *A. furfuraceus*, with white flowers, and *A. trigonus*, with yellow. The second group rarely outgrow a 4in (10cm) pot. Of these *A. kotschoubeyanus* (below, left) is most often seen. *A. agavoides* (still sometimes labelled *Neogomesia agavoides*) and *A. scapharostrus* are not for beginners.

Treating damaged roots
1. If a bought plant has damaged roots, they may rot, turning orange or brown at the base and becoming soft. Pare away rotting area into firm tissue with no more spots visible.

2. Dust liberally with hormone rooting powder containing a fungicide and leave for 2-3 weeks to dry thoroughly before repotting in fresh compost.

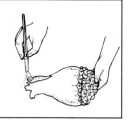

Ariocarpus lloydii has greyish-coloured, diamond-shaped tubercles which fit together like the sections of tortoise-shell but in spirals leading to the woolly centre.

A healthy plant will produce new wool at the centre and, if given plenty of sunlight, will flower in late summer or autumn. Flowers last about 3 days.

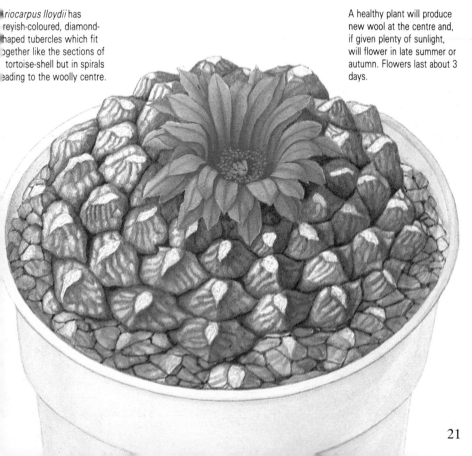

Arthrocereus

The cacti in this genus are columnar plants from Peru, Brazil and Argentina and grow to about 6in (15cm) tall. They produce long-tubed, scented flowers, mostly white, which open in the evening. There are about a dozen species to choose from, including those more often labelled *Pygmaeocereus* or *Setiechinopsis*, but except for *Arthrocereus* (or *Setiechinopsis*) *mirabilis* (p.23), most are only available from specialist cactus nurseries. Given a little extra care and attention, however, most of them will grow and flower well, producing flowers when they are only 3–4in (8–10cm) tall. They rarely outgrow a 4in (10cm) pot.

Arthrocereus rondonianus has pinkish-lilac flowers which unlike most in this genus, bloom in the daytime. Its finger thick stems grow up to 12in (30cm) long.

Light: Plenty of light is needed to keep the growth spiny and compact and to induce flowering; the sunniest spot is best.

Temperature: A minimum of 40°F (4°C) will suffice if they are kept dry in winter; keep below 100°F (38°C) and give fresh air in the summer months.

Water: Water about once a week in summer months. In early autumn, reduce watering to monthly and in the 3 coldest winter months, keep plant quite dry. Begin watering again in spring, gradually increasing to summer rate. Spray overhead monthly.

Feeding: Use a high potash fertilizer once a month in spring and summer (as for tomatoes).

Soil: Use about 40% coarse gritty sand (not builders' or seashore), 60% soil-less or good loam-based compost.

Repotting: Repot every year in the spring in fresh compost, leaving dry after repotting for 2 weeks. Use same size pot unless plant is outgrowing it. Be careful not to damage roots, and dust with a rooting powder containing a fungicide if you do, to combat rot.

Cleaning and pest control: A monthly forceful overhead spray with water will keep them dust-free. Add insecticide to the spray 2 or 3 times a year.

Other species: There is one reddish-lilac flowering species, *A. rondonianus*, with yellowish-brown, short spines on stems only finger-thick but growing to about 12in (30cm) long. *A. campos portoi* is difficult to grow well or indeed at all and is better grafted, and *A. microsphaericus* is not much better; both these species have white flowers. The 2 or 3 different *Pygmaeocereus* species are not so difficult, and *Arthrocereus* (or *Pygmaeocereus*) *bylesianus* or *akersii* are sometimes available from specialist nurseries. They have long-tubed, white flowers, freely produced if the plants get enough sunshine.

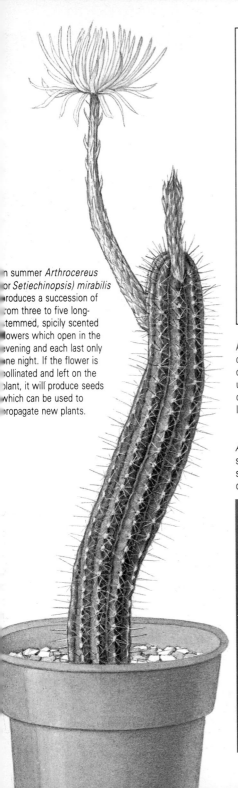

In summer *Arthrocereus* (or *Setiechinopsis*) *mirabilis* produces a succession of from three to five long-stemmed, spicily scented flowers which open in the evening and each last only one night. If the flower is pollinated and left on the plant, it will produce seeds which can be used to propagate new plants.

Collecting seeds

1. When flower dies and shrivels, its stem begins to swell as seeds develop.

2. After a few weeks it splits open to reveal a mass of black seeds.

3. Collect seeds carefully and prepare tray or small pot with soil-less or good loam-based No. 1 potting compost and top layer of grit. Sow seeds directly on surface.

As each flower bud develops, check each evening for the opening of the flowers. This usually starts about 8 to 10 o'clock in the evening and lasts through the night.

Arthrocereus (or *Pygmaeocereus*) *bylesianus* has long-stalked white flowers which appear two or three at a time in summer. They open in the evening when, in the wild, their colour and scent attract night-flying insects.

Astrophytum

Named for their star-like appearance, this small genus of cactus is one of the most popular with collectors. It consists of several very appealing, beautiful species, ranging in size from one growing barely above ground level and no more than 3–4in (8–10cm) wide, to another growing over 6ft (2m) tall in the wild. They come mainly from Mexico, although the smallest, *Astrophytum asterias*, also grows in Texas in the U.S.A. This one is rather difficult to keep as it is very susceptible to overwatering. *Astrophytum myriostigma* (p.25), the melon-sized 'Bishop's cap' cactus, is one of the easiest to grow.

Light: A sunny windowsill or greenhouse is necessary for best results, with no shading needed from the sun at all.

Temperature: Not less than 40°F (4°C); keep below 100°F (38°C) and give fresh air in the summer months.

Water: Be careful not to overwater at any time, especially *A. asterias*. Water about once every other week in the summer, or weekly for pots 3in (8cm) or less, making sure the pot has dried out from the previous watering. Keep dry in the winter months not watering in spring until the sun has gained some real strength and warmth.

Feeding: use high potash fertilizer (as used for tomatoes) once a month in summer.

Soil: Use 40% (60% for *A. asterias*) of coarse gritty sand (not builders' or sea-shore) in soil-less or good loam-based potting compost.

Repotting: Repot annually in the early years into large pots each year, until a 5in (13cm) pot is reached. Then every other year will do. Leave dry for a fortnight after potting.

Cleaning and pest control: Spray 2–3 times a year with an insecticide.

Other species: The small *A. asterias* has already been described as difficult to grow and

Astrophytum asterias is very sensitive to overwatering and is therefore difficult to grow well. Reaching eventually a size of about 3–4in (8–10cm) across, it produces flowers when it is only about 1½in (3cm), after about 5 years growth. It is spineless but has rows of white woolly areoles down the centre of each section, and an attractive pattern of white spots.

Astrophytum capricorne grows slowly to 6 or 8in (15 or 18cm) tall and produces its glorious yellow flowers with their red throat in the summer. It is covered with a tangle of long, curling, flexible spines like interlacing wire.

not recommended for beginners. It looks like a grey-green sea urchin, has no spines and is usually covered with a pattern of white spots. If you can keep it successfully, will produce pretty yellow flowers all through the summer. *A. capricorne* is another slow-growing species. The big fellow of the genus is *A. ornatum* which grows faster as well as larger than other species — in the wild 50 year old plants can be up to 6ft (2m). It has attractive flecking with yellow, stiff, sharp spines. It will usually produce flowers after 5–6 years, when it has grown to about 4in (10cm) tall and the same in diameter. In cultivation its usual maximum size is about 1ft (30cm).

strophytum myriostigma, ie 'Bishop's cap' cactus, is pineless, usually with five os, and covered with tiny white woolly flecks. After about ten years it will reach ie size of a small melon. A ealthy plant will have new ean growth appearing at ie top. Its sweet-scented owers appear all through ie summer, each lasting –3 days.

Never overwater Astrophytums. Be sure compost is thoroughly dried out from previous watering. If in doubt, err on the dry side.

Different Astrophytums have very different types of spine. *A ornatum* (1) has long, straight, rigid ones while *A capricorne's* (2) are curling and tangled. *A myriostigma* (3) has no spines but prominent felty pads instead.

1   2   3

Blossfeldia

This is the smallest cactus, and comes from Argentina and Bolivia. In cultivation they are invariably grafted, as they are extremely difficult to grow on their own roots for any length of time. A graft on a low-growing Echinopsis rootstock gives the best effect as little of the Echinopsis shows and the Blossfeldia looks almost as if it were growing on its own. They are often, however, sold grafted onto tall green triangular Hylocereus plants — known in the trade as 'lollipops'. Not only do they look rather unnatural growing like this, but the Hylocereus rootstock will not survive in temperatures below about 50–55°F (10–13°C), though other cacti will tolerate down to about 40°F (4°C) if kept dry. Grown on a graft, a plant such as *Blossfeldia liliputana* (p.27) will form dense clusters of tiny heads, each barely half an inch (1cm) or so across, spineless and covered with tiny, flat tufts of wool, from which the flowers emerge. The flowers are creamy-white and nearly as big as the plant bodies. A cluster in full flower is almost hidden by the blooms, so prolifically are they produced in the spring and early summer. They are not really a good candidate for raising from seed, and I know of only one or two very good seed-raisers who have ever succeeded in bringing plants from seed to maturity.

A Blossfeldia grafted on to a Hylocereus as favoured by some European and Japanese nurseries and known in the trade as 'lollipops'. Hylocereus are more tender than most other cacti so plants grafted onto their rootstock must be kept above 55°F (13°C) for safety.

Blossfeldia minima grown grafted onto an Echinopsis rootstock. If grown on their own roots, Blossfeldias are very difficult to cultivate successfully.

Light: A sunny position is needed to keep the heads tightly growing and the woolly clusters prominent, and to ensure flowering.
Temperature: If grafted on Hylocereus stock (see above) a minimum of 55°F (13°C) is needed for safety. On more usual cactus

Grafting

1. Remove top inch (2½cm) of the Echinopsis plant and a slice from the bottom of the Blossfeldia with a sharp, clean knife.

2. Immediately place the Blossfeldia's bottom cut surface firmly on the Echinopsis stump, making sure the rings near the centre of the stems overlap.

3. Hold firmly in place with an elastic band until new growth appears. Do not damage outer tissue with too tight or too narrow a band.

You can disguise the rootstock of a grafted plant with gravel so the Blossfeldia appears to be growing normally.

A healthy *Blossfeldia liliputana* (grown on a graft) has small heads no more than ½in (1cm) across, with prominent white tufts of wool close together. In spring and early summer, they produce masses of creamy-white flowers which almost hide the rest of the plant. Individual flowers last up to a week.

If growing a Blossfeldia on its own roots, spray weekly overhead but water the very open, gritty compost sparingly.

stock a minimum of 40°F (4°C) will suffice. Keep below 100°F (38°C) and give fresh air in summer months.

Water: Water about once a fortnight in late spring and summer, not at all in winter, and not more than once a month at other times. Spray overhead once a week all year round.

Feeding: Not necessary at all.

Soil: To keep growth in check because of the vigour of the grafting stock use gritty compost, with about half coarse, gritty sand (not builders' or seashore) to half soil-less or good loam-based No. 1 potting compost.

Repotting: Repot every other year in the spring into next size pot, and keep dry for a fortnight after repotting.

Cleaning and pest control: The frequent spraying will keep the plants dust-free and freshened. Add insecticide to the spray 3–4 times a year to keep pests at bay.

Other species: Differences are slight. If you have one you have them all.

27

Borzicactus

This genus includes similarly flowered but very differently shaped plants from a wide area of South America including Ecuador, Peru, Chile, Bolivia and Argentina. It includes many often sold under different genus names: those known as Oreocereus, the hairy old men of the Andes; Matucana, globular plants from Peru; Haageocereus and Seticereus, clustering, short columnar plants which grow slowly in cultivation, are densely spined in yellows and browns and flower when they are about 12in (30cm) tall; and the beautiful *Hildewintera aureispina*, a hanging, sprawling species with dense yellow spines and orange flowers. *Borzicactus trollii* (p.29) is one of the best known of the 'hairy' types.

Light: In the wild all grow in areas of strong sunlight. For good flowering and healthy spines they need the sunniest place you can find for them.

Temperature: Not less than 40°F (4°C) for safety; keep below 100°F (38°C) in summer and give fresh air when possible.

Water: Water weekly in spring and summer (fortnightly if in pot 4in (10cm) or more as these hold moisture for longer). Reduce watering to monthly in autumn and keep quite dry in winter.

Feeding: Feed in spring and summer with high potash fertilizer (as used for tomatoes) once a month.

Soil: Use 1 part of coarse, gritty sand (not builders' or seashore) to 2 parts soil-less or good loam-based No. 2 potting compost.

Repotting: Repot in next size pot in spring until 5in (13cm) pots reached. Then repot every other year or shake off old soil and replace plant in fresh soil in same size pot.

Cleaning and pest control: Spray with water if dusty and add an insecticide to spray 2 or 3 times a year.

Borzicactus (or *Seticereus*) *icosagonus* develops several thick stems (about 2in, 5cm) arching away from the base of the plant. They grow to about 18–24in (45–60cm) long and eventually hang downwards. The red-orange flowers appear from extra-bristly patches at the tips of the stems.

Borzicactus (or *Submatucana*) *intertextus* is a globular species with either red-orange or yellow flowers which are freely produced after it is about 2in (5cm) tall and wide. It grows to grapefruit size after about 5 or 6 years and seldom clusters though others of this type will form clumps.

Other species: There are several other white, hairy species (often known as *Oreocereus*), all very similar to one another. The globular *Matucana* types such as *Borzicactus* (or *Matucana*) *haynei* also tend to be similar in appearance with dense white or yellowish spines and red, occasionally pink flowers. The types known as *Submatucana* are more distinct from one another and flower more easily, especially *B.* (or *Submatucana*) *pauciostata*, a clustering cactus with red flowers, *B.* (or *Submatucana*) *madisoniorum*, with red flowers and *B.* (or *Submatucana*) *intertextus* with red or yellow flowers. *Haageocereus* and *Seticereus* species are grown mainly for their densely bristled stems but do occasionally flower. The most spectacular of all the Borzicacti is *B.* (or *Hildewintera*) *aureispina*, a hanging cactus with gold-spined curving stems.

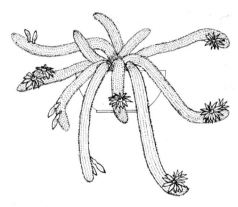

Borzicactus (Hildewintera) aureispina has thumb-thick stems up to 18in (50cm) long which are densely covered with short, stiff, bristle-like golden spines. The stems curve outwards and downwards from the centre like a golden fountain. Its salmon-pink flowers are produced in bursts along the mature stems throughout the spring and summer.

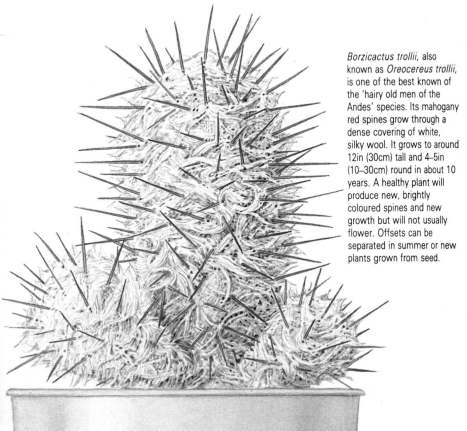

Borzicactus trollii, also known as *Oreocereus trollii*, is one of the best known of the 'hairy old men of the Andes' species. Its mahogany red spines grow through a dense covering of white, silky wool. It grows to around 12in (30cm) tall and 4–5in (10–30cm) round in about 10 years. A healthy plant will produce new, brightly coloured spines and new growth but will not usually flower. Offsets can be separated in summer or new plants grown from seed.

Chamaecereus

This name will survive for some time although most authorities acknowledge that the one species, *Chamaecereus sylvestrii* (p.31) is in fact an unusually shaped Lobivia (see p.52). It is often called the Peanut cactus because its stems look rather like unshelled peanuts. The stems grow to finger length, branching out as they grow. The new stems are only lightly attached and easily break off. The bright, vermilion red flowers appear all over the cactus in spring and summer. It comes from northern Argentina and is tolerant of low temperatures if dry. Of equal, perhaps more interest, are hybrids between *C. sylvestrii* and larger-flowered, more globular Lobivias. These, called 'Chamaelobivias' are like thick-stemmed versions of *C. sylvestrii* but with larger, differently coloured flowers.

Chamaelobivia 'Satsuma' has bright orange-yellow flowers opening from wool-covered buds. Chamaelobivia hybrids have thicker stems than the pure Chamaecereus cactus and are obtainable in a range of different colours.

Light: A sunny windowsill or greenhouse will ensure flowers and sturdy growth.
Temperature: For safety no lower than 40°F (4°C) though they can survive colder if quite dry; keep below 100°F (38°C) in summer and give fresh air.
Water: Keep dry in winter, water once a week in the summer, and about once a fortnight in the spring and autumn.
Feeding: Feed 2 or 3 times in the growing season (spring and summer) with high potash fertilizer (as used for tomatoes). Too much fertilizer makes them grow larger but produce fewer flowers.
Soil: Use an open, gritty soil, with 1 part coarse, gritty sand (not builders' or seashore) to 2 parts loam-based No. 2 potting compost or soil-less compost.
Repotting: This is difficult without the plant breaking up, as the stems are lightly attached to each other; the hybrids have a stronger connection. Repot every year for

Chamaelobivia 'Shot Scarlet' is one of the best hybrids, making thick, compact stems with deep crimson flowers flushed with purple. It is a hybrid between *C. sylvestrii* and *Lobivia backebergiana*.

Taking cuttings
Cuttings taken after
flowering root easily. Cut
whole stem where it grows
from plant, dust with
hormone rooting powder
containing fungicide and
leave to dry for at least 2
days before planting on
fresh compost.

the first 4 years into next size half-pot or
pan, then every other year will be enough.
Broken stems will root easily to make new
plants.

Cleaning and pest control: Spray with water
if dusty and add insecticide to the spray 2 or
3 times a year during the growing season;
these plants are especially susceptible to
damage by red spider mite.

Other species: *C. sylvestrii* is the only true
species, but some of the hybrids on the
market are well worthwhile. Many are
merely larger, red-flowering forms, but
some good colour breaks have been
produced, with yellow, purple-red, pale
orange and varying shades of crimson:
Chamaelobivia 'Kent Sunrise' has yellow
flowers with pink outer petals; *C.* 'Shot
Scarlet' has deep crimson flowers flushed
purple; *C.* 'Satsuma' is orange and
C. 'Pegler' has purple flowers.

Chamaecereus sylvestrii
produces bright red flowers
in spring and summer, each
lasting four to five days. A
healthy plant should have
short, sturdy stems with
good spines. If stems are
long and floppy or pale rather
than mid-green to brownish
red, they need more light.

Cleistocactus

This is a widespread genus of cactus from South America which gives the collector a chance to obtain flowers at a relatively small size on columnar plants. Most other columnar cacti are taller than their owners before flowers are likely to appear! Cleistocactus species vary from tall, column-like plants with stems as thick as your arm, to narrow, pencil-thin, sprawling stems which in the wild clamber through shrubs or over hillsides. They are noted for their dense, needle-like spines which completely clothe the stems, in colours varying from pure, glassy white to browns and yellows. Their flowers are mainly red, orange and yellow, tube-shaped with a tiny opening at the end through which, in the wild, long-tongued pollinators such as hummingbirds probe in search of nectar. *Cleistocactus strausii* (p.33) is the most commonly sold species.

A group of Cleistocacti growing in a private garden (Lotus Land) in California. In good conditions these plants may grow up to 10ft (over 3m) tall, making a spectacular display.

Light: The more sunlight these plants can be given the more dense the spines will be and the greater the likelihood of flowers.

Temperature: Not less than 40°F (4°C); keep below 100°F (38°C) in summer and give fresh air whenever possible.

Water: Weekly in summer, less often for plants in 6in (15cm) pots or larger as these hold moisture for longer. Leave dry in winter. Water monthly in spring and autumn.

Feeding: Feed once a month in spring and summer with high potash fertilizer (as used for tomatoes).

Soil: Use soil-less compost or 2 parts good loam-based No. 2 potting compost (No. 3 for large plants) with 1 part coarse, gritty sand (not builders' or seashore) added.

Repotting: Repot each spring until 6in (15cm) pots are reached, when every other year will do. Get help when the plants grow too big to handle with ease. They may grow 5–6ft (up to 2m) or more. Avoid touching the spiny stems altogether for fear of damage to the brittle spines. Cut out old stems which have stopped growing.

Cleaning and pest control: Spray with water to keep dust-free; add an insecticide to the water 2 or 3 times a year to combat pests.

Other species: A good alternative to *C. strausii* is *C. ritteri*, with thinner, white-spined stems and yellow flowers. *C. santacruzensis* will flower at only about 8in (20cm) on pencil-thin stems with long spines; the flowers are red and yellow. An unusual, pendant species with yellow-brown, soft spines completely hiding the stems is *C. vulpis-cauda* (the name means 'fox-tail'), which has red flowers produced on and off for over 6 months; it is a good plant for a hanging pot or basket.

C.vulpis-cauda is a good candidate for a hanging basket. It is best to use a special plastic pot with saucer attached and chains for suspending it. The plant can then be potted directly into the container with the usual compost. Check regularly for moisture as hanging containers dry out more quickly than standing ones.

Cleistocactus strausii flowers when it is five or six years old, and about 12in (30cm) tall. The deep red flowers appear during the spring and summer months, each lasting from four to five days. A healthy plant will make several inches of fresh growth each season, producing brightly coloured spines at the growing point of the stem.

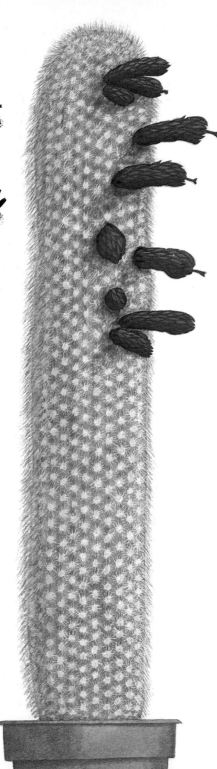

Removing old stems

1. When secondary stems begin to grow from base of plant, first stem sometimes gradually turns brown and withers.

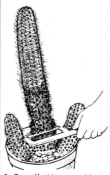

2. Cut off old stem with a hacksaw as near to soil level as possible and dust cut surface liberally with hormone rooting powder containing fungicide.

3. When cut surface is dry, repot in centre of new pot large enough to hold all roots and the remains of the old stump. This can be disguised with a layer of gravel.

Copiapoa

These cacti come from the very arid stony coastal deserts of Chile, where rainfall is almost non-existent. Their water needs are often only supplied by the heavy sea mists which roll in from the coast. Condensation on the cactus spines and on the ground around them keeps them just alive. Some of the larger species such as *Copiapoa cinerea* grow up to 52in (130cm) in the wild but take 20 years to reach maturity and flower; others, such as *C. calderana* may flower when smaller. The ones more suitable for indoor growth, produce their flowers after 2–3 years, when they are about the size of golf balls. *C. montana* (p.35), a more columnar plant, flowers when it is about 2in (5cm) tall. All have similar flowers, with stamens fanning over the inside of the yellow petals.

Copiapoa haseltoniana offsets when quite young, eventually forming large clumps of olive-green stems and creamy-coloured spines. Flowers are not easily induced – a good sunny position gives the best chance.

Light: They need high light intensity on the sunniest windowsill or in an unshaded greenhouse.

Temperature: Keep above 40°F (4°C) in winter but in summer they will stand very high temperatures provided that there is sufficient ventilation to keep the air circulating.

Copiapoa calderana grows quite slowly but will flower when about 2in (5cm) tall. The appearance of copious wool at the top is usually a sign that the plant is about to flower.

Water: Do not overwater at any time: in the wild they survive on very little. Keep dry in winter and start watering only in late spring. In spring and summer water once a fortnight, allowing soil to dry out between waterings. Stop watering completely in early autumn.

Feeding: Feed once a month with high potash fertilizer (as used for tomatoes) in spring and summer.

Soil: Use 1 part soil-less or good loam-based No. 2 or No. 3 potting compost with 2 parts coarse, gritty sand (not seashore or builders').

Repotting: Repot every year into next size

pot until they are in 5in (13cm) pots. Then every other year will do. If roots have not outgrown the container, replace plant in same pot with fresh soil.

Cleaning and pest control: Spray monthly in spring and summer with water to keep dust-free and incorporate an insecticide to combat pests 2 or 3 times a year.

Other species: *C. barquitensis* and *C. hypogaea* both produce yellow flowers when their khaki-brown bodies have grown to about golf-ball size. After some years they produce offsets and form many-headed clumps. Their short black spines have wool-like strands stretched between them and the flower buds emerge from a woolly centre. *C. tenuissima* has dark brown, almost black bodies, with tiny fine black spines. It is smaller than the first two mentioned but flowers freely. *C. humilis* is columnar, like *C. montana* (below) and is the only other small species commonly available. Of the larger types, *C. cinerea* and *C. haseltoniana* are sometimes available but will seldom flower in cultivation and if imported from the wild are difficult to establish.

Copiapoa montana grows to 3–4in (7–10cm) tall and 2in (5cm) wide, increasing by about 1in (½cm) a year. It flowers at about 2in (5cm), producing 5–6 yellow flowers over a period of a week or more in the summer. It has long black spines and should have copious wool in the growing point at its tip and down its ribs.

Most Copiapoas have tuberous roots. Be careful not to damage them when repotting.

Coryphantha

Coryphanthas are not often found in shops, but are obtainable from specialist nurserymen. They are slow-growing, taking 5–6 years to fill a 4–5in (10–13cm) pot, with often strong spines, lots of white wool at the top of the plant and all but a few have large, silky, yellow flowers produced after they are about 2in (5–6cm) across. Some will slowly offset and make clumps after 5 or 6 years, others stay solitary, becoming columnar in time, but usually they remain globular for some years. They come from a wide area in Mexico and the southern United States, with one species as far north as British Columbia and southern Canada. This is *Coryphantha vivipara* (p.37), which produces fringed, pinkish flowers in summer if kept in a good sunny position. It is susceptible to overwatering and should not be put in too large a pot where moisture may stay around the roots for too long.

Coryphantha georgii is a species taller than it is broad, with outstanding slender, sharp needle-like spines. Its pale yellow flowers are produced after it is about 3 or 4in (8-10cm) tall.

Light: Maximum light is needed to keep growth compact and induce flowers.

Temperature: 40°F (4°C) in winter will suffice; keep below 100°F (38°F) in summer and give fresh air when possible.

Water: Moderate watering is needed in spring and summer, watering about once a fortnight or more often for small pots (3in, 8cm or less) which dry out quickly. Keep dry from late autumn to spring.

Feeding: Feed once a month with high potash fertilizer (as used for tomatoes) in spring and summer.

Soil: Use open, gritty compost, 1 part coarse, gritty sand (not builders' or seashore) in 2 parts soil-less or good loam-based No. 2 potting compost.

Repotting: Repot every year into next size pots until 5in (13cm) pots are reached, when every other year will do.

Coryphantha guerkeana has pale yellow or whitish flowers edged with pink. When fully open they completely cover the plant body.

A healthy *Coryphantha vivipara* makes fresh growth of bright new spines or wool at the centre and should flower in summer after it is about 2 or 3in (5–6cm) in diameter, that is at about 5 or 6 years old from seed. Flowers last for about a week.

Coryphanthas should be watered when the pot dries out in spring and summer but kept dry from late autumn to spring. Keep them in as sunny position as possible to ensure flowering and good, strong growth.

Cleaning and pest control: Do not spray the woolly-topped species overhead, or the wool is liable to become discoloured. If spraying is necessary to combat pests, brush the wool up lightly when dry. Better still, add systemic insecticide to water.

Other species: A group looking very different from *C. vivipara* have large, fat, shining green tubercles and strong curving spines. Most Coryphanthas have yellow flowers but a few have pink or red. *C. andreae*, *C. bumamma*, *C. elephantidens* and *C. guerkeana* are good examples of the large-tubercled species. There are many others available from specialist nurseries from time to time; some, such as *C. georgii*, are more columnar, or with finer spines, solitary or clustering, the range is wide.

Offsets
1. Many species produce offsets around the base. Cut them off at their narrowest point with a clean, sharp knife.

2. Dust with hormone rooting powder containing fungicide and leave to dry for at least 2 days. Then plant in fresh compost. Keep them in a light place but do not water for 2–3 weeks, when roots will have started to develop.

Echinocactus

These are the largest of the globular cacti, with some reaching about 5ft (1½m) across in the wild in Mexico and the southern United States. In cultivation they will take 5 or 6 years to get beyond a 6 or 7in (15–18cm) pot, and few will produce flowers under the size of a football. But they are handsome plants at any size, and are often seen for sale. As they get older their true beauty emerges and the spines get more and more strong and lend ferocious beauty to the plants. Kept growing vigorously they will eventually become among the most prominent in the collection.

The most popular species is *Echinocactus grusonii*, commonly known as the Golden barrel cactus. It is one of the most beautifully spined cacti there is, with stiff, bright golden yellow spines like sword-blades densely covering the globular plant.

Echinocactus horizonthalonius is difficult to grow unless kept very well drained in a good, sunny position. It is best to water on bright, sunny days and to allow the pot to dry out thoroughly between waterings. When not in flower, a healthy plant will produce fresh wool in the centre. Flowers are produced in the summer months and last a week or more each.

Light: Maximum light is needed to produce strong spines.

Temperature: A minimum of 45°F (7°C) is needed, with preferably 50°F (10°C) for *E. grusonii* to prevent 'cold' marks, brown unsightly spotting. Give fresh air in summer and keep below 100°F (38°C).

Water: Weekly in summer until plants large enough for 5in (13cm) pots, then fortnightly. Keep dry from late autumn to spring.

Feeding: Feed every month in summer with high potash fertilizer (as used for tomatoes).

Soil: Use 1 part coarse, gritty sand (not builders' or seashore) to 2 parts of soil-less or good loam-based No. 2 potting compost (No. 3 for larger plants).

Repotting: Use gloves to protect your hands and avoid breaking the spines when repotting. This should be done every year into next size pot until in 6 or 7in (15 or

A healthy *Echinocactus grusonii* is one which makes plenty of bright new spines in the summer and is not marked with brown cold marks after the winter. It is unlikely to flower in cultivation and needs to be at least the size of a football before any flowers will appear; but its beautiful yellow spines make a splendid year-round display.

Spraying occasionally overhead keeps the spines clean and bright yellow. Feeding promotes strong growth and healthy spines.

Mealy bug

1. Dab and remove woolly patches with small paintbrush or cotton bud dipped in methylated spirits, and spray with diluted malathion, repeating after 10 days if not clear.

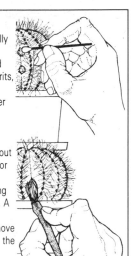

2. Brush all dead pests out from between the ribs, or moulds may set up rot. Use a typewriter cleaning brush with long bristles. A toothpick or broken matchstick helps to remove any bugs from between the spines.

18cm) pot, then every other year will be enough.

Cleaning and pest control: Spray with water if dusty and incorporate an insecticide 2 or 3 times a year to combat pests.

Other species: A white-spined form of *E. grusonii* is available. It needs to be at least football size before the yellow flowers appear. Few others are seen except for *E. horizonthalonius*, from southern U.S.A. and Mexico. This flowers when quite small (3in, 8cm or so) with lovely pink blooms on blue-green stems with strong, curved black or brown spines. A difficult plant, it is one for the experienced grower rather than the beginner.

Brown cold marks are unsightly but not fatal. Do not cut them out or the plant may be damaged.

Echinocereus

Some of the largest, most sumptuous flowers of the cactus family are found in this genus. It comes from a wide area of the southern U.S.A. and Mexico, mostly forming large clumps half a metre or more across, of cylindrical stems up to 8–12in (20–30cm) tall. Many will flower at about 4in (10cm) tall and are content with shallow half-pots or pans though some have larger, tuberous roots and need deeper containers. Check which type of roots the cactus has when repotting. They fall into five main types. The larger, long-spined species such as *Echinocereus fendleri* are not easy to flower in cultivation but may grow up to 18in (50cm) across. In the wild they may reach as much as 3ft (1m). Better for flowering is the sprawling group which contains *E. blanckii* and *E. papillosus*, or the group with short spines neatly arranged like primitive combs down the ribs, such as *E. pectinatus*. These have mainly large, pink flowers, produced when the plants are only small. They rarely outgrow a 7in (18cm) pot. Another group has small, greenish-yellow or rusty-red flowers. This includes *E. davisii*, which flowers when only about 1in (2–3cm) tall. The last group consists of a few small, nearly globular species such as *E. pulchellus* which grow only about an inch (2½cm) a year but produce masses of flowers. *E. pulchellus* itself has strong, short spines in star-like clusters, often smothering itself with 20 or more blooms on one 2in (5cm) head.

Echinocereus triglochidiatus has thick, squat stems and is a very variably spined species. Although it flowers readily in the wild, it needs a sunny position to encourage flower production in cultivation. The bright red flowers, each lasting about a fortnight, are thick-textured and waxy.

Light: Give maximum light on the sunniest windowsill or in a greenhouse.
Temperature: Keep above 40°F (4°C) for

safety. Give fresh air in summer and keep below 100°F (38°C) if possible.

Water: Water weekly in summer, fortnightly in spring and autumn. Keep dry in winter.

Feeding: Feed with high potash fertilizer (as used for tomatoes) in spring and summer.

Soil: Use 1 part of coarse, gritty sand (not builders' or seashore) to 2 parts of soil-less or good loam-based No. 2 potting compost (No. 3 for larger plants).

Repotting: Do not put small plants in over-large pots; their roots should fill the pot. Repot every year into next size pot. If plant has very shallow root system, use a half-pot or pan. For plants that are growing strongly, repot each year into next size until 7in (18cm) reached, then every other year unless it is obviously outgrowing its container.

Cleaning and pest control: Spray with water if dusty and include an insecticide 2 or 3 times a year to combat pests.

Other species: The sprawling group is well represented by *E. blanckii* and plants are available in each of the other main groups. Larger, hard-to-flower species include *E. brandegei*, *E. maritimus* and *E. triglochidiatus*. The small 'comb' cacti include *E. purpureus*, *E. melanocentrus*, *E. reichenbachii*. The small-flowered group includes *E. chloranthus*, *E. viridiflorus*, and *E. russanthus* while the free-flowering globular species include *E. knippelianus*, with dark green stem and wispy, easily knocked off spines. It has large pink flowers with a deeper pink midstripe. *E. subinermis*, in this group, has beautiful large butter yellow flowers.

Echinocereus papillosus is a species that flowers readily in cultivation and will grow quickly to fill a 7 or 8in (18-20cm) pan with its shallow roots. Its flowers are a pale, silky yellow with red throats and appear over a 2 or 3 week period in late spring or early summer, individual flowers lasting about 7 to 10 days.

Echinocereus blanckii belongs to the sprawling group of Echinocereus. It spreads to fill a 10in (25cm) pan but has shallow, fibrous roots so does not need a deep container. Its bright purple flowers appear for about a month in spring and early summer, each lasting for a week or ten days.

41

Echinopsis

These are popular, night-flowering globular cacti whose flowers open in the evening to fade by the following morning. Most have white or pale pink flowers, with tubes 4–5in (10–12cm) long but some, such as *Echinopsis aurea* (p.43), have attractive yellow blooms. They grow to 2½–3in (6–8cm) tall and about 2½in (6cm) wide or larger. They offset freely and since the offsets root easily when they are removed, new young plants are widely available. Many will survive a winter outside if frost is not too severe but are better kept indoors. They come from a wide area of South America.

The name Pseudolobivia is sometimes applied to some of these plants and in addition Echinopsis species have been crossed with Lobivias to produce what are known as Echinobivias.

Echinobivia 'Ginn and Orange'. Echinobivias have shorter flower tubes (2½–3in 6–8cm) than normal Echinopsis plants but produce more blooms. Other good Echinobivias are E. 'Stars and Stripes', E. 'Mary Patricia', E. 'Peach Monach' and E. 'Sunset'.

Light: For best results, keep in the sunniest position possible. If no flowers appear, the light is probably too dull, perhaps filtered through a net curtain.

Temperature: Although these plants have been known to survive mild frost, they prefer a temperature above 40°F (4°C). Keep below 100°F (38°C) and give fresh air in summer when possible.

Water: Weekly in the summer, fortnightly in spring and autumn or if the plants are in pots of more than 5in (13cm); keep dry in winter.

Feeding: Feed every month in spring and summer with high potash fertilizer (as used for tomatoes).

Soil: Use 2 parts soil-less or good loam-based No. 2 potting compost (No. 3 for large plants) with 1 part coarse, gritty sand (not builders' or seashore).

Repotting: Repot every year into next size pot until they are in 5in (13cm) pots, when every other year will be sufficient. Then, unless plant is outgrowing its pot, repot in same size container with fresh soil.

Cleaning and pest control: Spray with water once a month to keep dust-free and incorporate an insecticide 2 or 3 times a year to combat pests.

Other species: *E. callichroma* has yellow flowers like *E. aurea* (right) but most have white or pinkish flowers. Some which have become available in recent years are worth looking out for: *E. obrepanda*, *E. kratochviliana* and *E. subdenudata* have white flowers and *E. frankii*, *E. cardenasiana* and *E. kermesina* have pink to red-violet ones. *E. kermesina* (sometimes known as Pseudolobivia) has a light green body with yellowish-brown spines. Unlike most other Echinopsis species, it produces its long-tubed flowers from the centre. The many hybrid Echinobivias come in shades of pink, red, orange and yellow.

Offsets

Offsets produced around base root easily. Remove with sharp knife when 1in (2½cm) high. Dust base with hormone rooting powder containing fungicide, dry off for 2 days and plant in fresh dry compost. Do not water for 2 weeks.

Echinopsis cardenasiana's magnificent flowers dwarf the plant's small body. The plant shown here is about 3in (7½cm) wide but they begin to produce flowers when they are only 2in (5cm) wide.

Echinopsis species come from Argentina, Bolivia, Paraguay, Uruguay and Brazil. They can stand low temperatures but are best kept above 40°F (4°C).

If your Echinopsis does not flower, move it into the sunniest possible position. Do not keep in light filtered through a net curtain.

Echinopsis aurea is usually a shining, healthy dark green, with vertical ribs and clusters of sharp spines. It grows to about 4in (10cm) indoors and flowers after 3–4 years, when it is 1½–2in (4–5cm) tall. Its yellow flowers appear in late spring, either all together or over a week or two, lasting 1 or 2 days each. The tubes from which the flowers appear are hairy and grow out from the side of the plant, just above a cluster of spines.

43

Epiphyllum

Most so-called Epiphyllums are not true Epiphyllums at all but are hybrids of hybrids whose true origins are rarely known. They are nevertheless very popular because of their large, exotically coloured blooms with their prominent swoop of stamens in the centre. The flowers give the plants their popular name of Orchid cacti and come in all shades of white, yellow, orange, red (the most common), pink or purple and combinations of these colours.

They have been bred from jungle cacti which, in nature, grow in trees as epiphytes, obtaining nourishment from the rotting vegetation accumulated among the branches, into which they root. They should therefore be treated rather differently from the desert cacti. The most commonly seen is the red-flowered *Epiphyllum ackermannii*.

Epiphyllum 'Sarabande' with its large white flowers and yellow outer sepals is one of the most attractive hybrids. Others often found are E. 'Deutsche Kaiserin', with soft pink flowers, and E. 'Reward' with yellow blooms.

Light: Like all cacti, they need a good light position for best results. A sunny windowsill is ideal. If in a greenhouse in summer, shade lightly but give full light in winter when flower buds are forming.

Temperature: Keep above 40°F (4°C) in winter and below 100°F (38°C) in summer; give fresh air when possible in summer.

Water: These plants need some water all year round. If kept below 45°F (7°C) in winter they should be almost dry, watered every 4–6 weeks, but in summer they need watering once or twice a week to keep the soil moist. Do not allow them to stand in water.

Feeding: Feed every week in spring and summer with high potash fertilizer (as used for tomatoes).

Soil: Use soil-less composts with no grit or sand added. Some growers prefer lime-free or 'ericaceous' composts which are more like the leaf debris in which the plants grow in the wild.

Repotting: Repot annually into next size pot, if plant is growing well. Pot should be large enough to take the root-ball comfortably with room for fresh soil to be added around it. Strong growers will fill 9in (23cm) or bigger pots but when they get to this size can be replaced each year in the same sized pot with fresh compost. Make sure there is good drainage in the pot.

Cleaning and pest control: Wipe the leaf-like stems clean with a damp cloth if they are dusty and spray them once a month to keep them clean. Incorporate an insecticide 2 or 3 times a year to combat pests and a fungicide to prevent brown or orange spotting.

Other species: The choice of flower colours is endless and thousands have been named in the last fifty years. There are a few cactus nurseries who specialize in these plants and it is worth a visit in spring and early summer when they are flowering to choose from the great variety available.

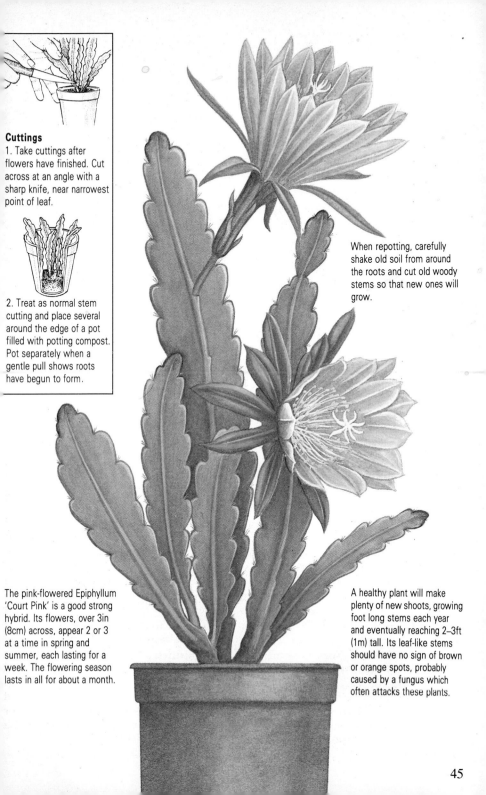

Cuttings

1. Take cuttings after flowers have finished. Cut across at an angle with a sharp knife, near narrowest point of leaf.

2. Treat as normal stem cutting and place several around the edge of a pot filled with potting compost. Pot separately when a gentle pull shows roots have begun to form.

When repotting, carefully shake old soil from around the roots and cut old woody stems so that new ones will grow.

The pink-flowered Epiphyllum 'Court Pink' is a good strong hybrid. Its flowers, over 3in (8cm) across, appear 2 or 3 at a time in spring and summer, each lasting for a week. The flowering season lasts in all for about a month.

A healthy plant will make plenty of new shoots, growing foot long stems each year and eventually reaching 2–3ft (1m) tall. Its leaf-like stems should have no sign of brown or orange spots, probably caused by a fungus which often attacks these plants.

Espostoa

These white, woolly cacti, like small cotton-wool columns, come from the Andes in southern Ecuador and northern Peru. *Espostoa melanostele* (p.47) is an attractive example. They are slow-growing in cultivation, as in the wild, growing only about 2in (5cm) a year at most when they are young. In the wild they flower when they are about 3–4ft (1m) tall, producing an extra-thick woolly area called a cephalium at one side of the top of the stem, from which the flowers appear. Although this is very unlikely to happen in the home, they make handsome plants, the new wool produced each year swathing the top of the stem in white swirls. The wool becomes thicker as the plant ages, eventually entirely covering the stem. But beware of the spines which are half hidden by the wool and are needle sharp.

Espostoa superba produces some wool at the top of its stem but is much less woolly than other species. It grows to 2 or 3ft (1m) tall in 10 to 15 years and like other Espostoa species is unlikely to flower in the home.

Light: In the wild these cacti grow at high altitudes with high light intensity so they need maximum sunshine all the year round, on a sunny windowsill or in a greenhouse. If they do not receive enough sunshine, they will become elongated and less woolly.

Temperature: Keep above 40°F (4°C) in winter and below 100°F (38°C) in summer. Give fresh air whenever possible in summer.

Water: In spring and summer water about once a week, once a fortnight for larger plants. Always test compost. In dull weather it will not dry out so quickly and may become waterlogged. In autumn reduce watering to once every 3 weeks, then once a month. If plant is in a big pot (9in, 23cm or more) stop watering altogether in autumn to allow compost to dry out. Keep dry in winter, starting to water again in spring.

Normal stems of *Espostoa ritteri* growing from a cristate plant. Cristate plants produce multiple growing points instead of a single column, giving a ribbon-like or fan-like effect.

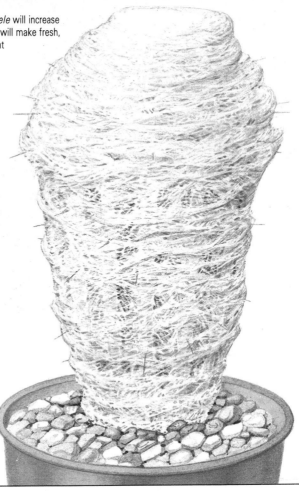

A healthy *Espostoa melanostele* will increase steadily if slowly in height and will make fresh, white wool at the growing point each year. As the plants get to more than 6in (15cm) the wool will get thicker and thicker, growing in a swirl around the top of the cactus.

Flowers are unlikely in the home; the plant needs to be 3 or 4ft (a metre) tall and may take more than 15 years to reach this size.

Feeding will encourage quick clean growth and thicker wool.

Support the plant with a stick and a tie made of soft, loose material after repotting. Remove as soon as plant is settled, to avoid marking it.

Lightly brushing the wool will fluff it up and improve the plant's appearance. If it becomes dark and dirty do not shampoo, in spite of some advocates of this drastic measure: brush lightly with a very small amount of detergent in warm water.

For best-looking plants, repot annually to help keep plant growing quickly.

Feeding: Feed once a month in spring and summer with a high potash fertilizer (as used for tomatoes).

Soil: Use 1 part coarse gritty sand (not builders' or seashore) to 2 parts soil-less or good loam-based No. 2 potting compost (No. 3 mixture for large plants). Good drainage essential.

Repotting: Repot every year in spring into next size pot until in 5in (13cm) size. Then repot every other year. Once plant is about 2ft (60cm) tall and in a 9in (23cm) pot, keep it in the same sized container. Remove from pot each year to shake off old compost. Replace with new compost. Repotting these large plants is a two-person job.

Cleaning and pest control: Give an occasional light brushing to bring up the fluffiness of the wool. Spraying will make it look matt and unsightly. Pests are best treated with systemic insecticides, which are taken up through the roots, as the wool is difficult to penetrate with sprays and protects the pests from contact sprays. Add insecticides to the water when watering 2 or 3 times a year or if pests occur.

Other species: All the available species look very similar though some are less woolly than others. *E. ritteri* has reddish spines and sparse white wool and *E. superba* is also a less woolly one. Woolly species, apart from *E. melanostele*, are *E. lanata*, *E. sericata*, *E. nana*, *E. mirabilis* and some others. All are essentially similar plants.

Ferocactus

These are the Barrel cacti of the American and Mexican deserts, said to provide the thirsty traveller with water from their succulent interior. It would be a bitter drink, but the fable persists. Many of these plants in the wild grow to massive, thick columns taller than a man, but there are a few of more modest size which will flower in cultivation. With the large species the likelihood of getting them to flowering size is remote, unless you start when you are very young for they may take 15–20 years to reach maturity. They are often worth growing for the beauty of their fierce spines. The smaller growing species such as *Ferocactus macrodiscus* (p.49) will produce flowers when they are about 4in (10cm) in diameter, after 6–8 years.

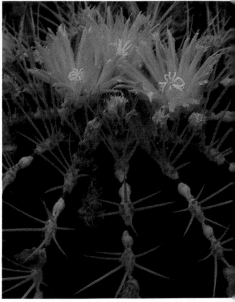

Ferocactus glaucescens has a blue-green body with bright yellow spines. Often grown for its form and colour alone, it will flower when it is about 8in (20cm) in diameter, after about 10 years growth.

Light: Maximum light is needed for good strong growth of plants and spines, as well as for the possibility of flowers in the smaller species. Keep on the sunniest windowsill or, ideally, in a greenhouse.

Ferocactus gracilis has wonderfully bright red, fiercely hooked spines. The fiery red flowers are unlikely in cultivation until the plant is a foot (30cm) or more tall, which will take 12 or 15 years good growth.

Temperature: For safety keep above 40°F (4°C) in winter; keep below 100°F (38°C) in summer, and give fresh air when possible.

Water: Water in spring and summer weekly (fortnightly for larger plants). Always make sure compost has dried out from previous watering before adding more. Tail off watering in the autumn to once every 3 weeks or a month and keep dry in winter.

Feeding: Use a high potash fertilizer in spring and summer about once a month (as used for tomatoes).

Soil: Use 2 parts of coarse, gritty sand (not builders' or seashore) to 3 parts of soil-less or good loam-based No. 2 potting compost (No. 3 for large plants). Good drainage essential.

Repotting: Repot annually in the early years into next size larger pot in spring. When 7in

(18cm) pot is reached repot every other year, or replace in same sized pot with fresh soil, after carefully shaking the old soil off the roots. Do not water for a fortnight after repotting.

Cleaning and pest control: Spray every week with water to dilute the sticky nectar which oozes from the areoles. Incorporate an insecticide 2 or 3 times a year to combat pests.

Other species: Large species (football size) worth growing for their spines are *F. gracilis* or *F. acanthodes*, noted for their colourful red or yellow dense, strong spines and *F. glaucescens*. For flowers on smaller growing species there are three that are outstanding: *F. macrodiscus* (below), *F. viridescens* and *F. fordii*. All will be 6–8 years old by the time they reach flowering size. *F. latispinus* grows more slowly but flowers at about the same size (3–4in, 8–10cm). It has pink flowers and extremely thick hooked spines.

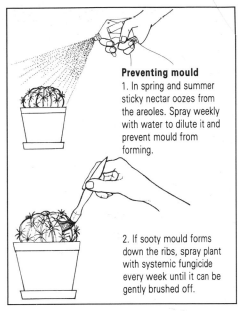

Preventing mould
1. In spring and summer sticky nectar oozes from the areoles. Spray weekly with water to dilute it and prevent mould from forming.

2. If sooty mould forms down the ribs, spray plant with systemic fungicide every week until it can be gently brushed off.

Ferocactus macrodiscus has curving spines which are red when young, fading to yellowish buff with time. It is low-growing and flowers when it has grown to 4 or 5in (10-12cm) wide, after 6–8 years.

A healthy plant will make fresh bright coloured spines each year and will slowly increase in size. It is especially important to give the plant as much sun as possible in the winter to encourage the formation of flower buds.

Gymnocalycium

This very popular genus of cacti comes from a wide area of South America, in Bolivia, Paraguay, Brazil, Uruguay and Argentina. It consists mainly of single-stemmed, globular, strong-spined plants, freely flowering at a few inches across, and, except for a few species, rarely needing more than a 5in (13cm) pot. *Gymnocalycium baldianum* (p.51) has red flowers but other species may have flowers coloured green, yellow, red, pink and most commonly white, often flushed with pink or red. They are readily obtainable from specialist nurseries, and are almost indestructible, putting up with a good deal of inattention.

Gymnocalycium bruchii is easy to grow and flower and will rapidly form clumps of stems, each no more than about ¾in (2cm) tall and wide. The flowers appear in early summer, 2 or 3 on each head and on a large clump there may be a hundred or more. The plant here is in a 5in (13cm) pan.

Light: As with most cacti they need a light position on a sunny windowsill. If grown in a greenhouse they need a little shading during the sunniest months.

Temperature: Keep above 40°F (4°C) for safety; keep below 100°F (38°C) and give fresh air in summer if possible.

Water: Water about once a fortnight in spring and summer, weekly in hot weather. Check compost before watering to make sure it has dried out. Tail off watering in autumn to once a month and keep dry in winter.

Feeding: Use a high potash fertilizer once a month in spring and summer (as used for tomatoes).

Soil: Use 1 part of coarse, gritty sand (not builders' or seashore) to 2 parts of soil-less or good loam-based No. 2 potting compost.

Repotting: These plants are best repotted every year into the next size pot when they are young and even when they have reached their maximum size and are in a 5in (13cm) pot they should be repotted into fresh soil each year. At this size they can be replaced in the same container. Do not water for 2 weeks after repotting.

Cleaning and pest control: Spray with water if dusty and incorporate an insecticide 2 or 3 times a year to combat pests.

Other species: For larger growing ones, *G. buenekeri* is one of the best. It makes a globular plant with few, fat ribs of matt green. The spines are well spaced out and lie close to the body, apparently more for adornment then defence. When about 10 years old it will be 6in (15cm) tall, the same across and will produce half a dozen or so robust offsets. Its flowers are a lovely shade of pink. Another large grower, but a solitary not an offsetting type, is *G. saglione*. This is magnificently spiny with curving red or yellow spines and pale pink flowers. There are many smaller growers and a good selection in addition to *G. baldianum* (right) is, *G. andreae* or *G. leeanum* (yellow flowers), *G. bicolor* (pink/white flowers), *G. bruchii* (clusters of small heads with wispy spines and pink and white flowers). *G. friedrichii* (reddish purple body and pink flowers).

Gymnocalycium bicolor, named for its two-coloured black and white spines, is a robust grower, reaching about 4in (10cm) across in 5 years or so, and wider than it is high. Its large shell-pink flowers are produced after about 3 years, when it is some 2in (5cm) wide.

Growing from seed

1. Sow seed thinly in spring on surface of prepared tray. Tap sides of tray to settle seed.

2. Water from base with fungicide diluted as for 'damping off' of seedlings until surface is damp.

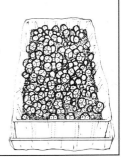

3. Cover with polythene and leave in light (not sunlight) at 70°F (21°C). Do not water again unless condensation on polythene becomes patchy or dries. Prick out after 6 months into 2in (5cm) pots or ½in (2cm) apart in tray.

Gymnocalycium baldianum has bright red flowers which appear when it is 2–3 years old and only about 2in (5cm) across. The flowers come over a period in the summer, opening from dark green buds at the top of the plant. They each last about a week.

Gymocalyciums are best kept out of midday summer sun. If in a greenhouse, provide some shade during the hottest months.

These cacti are not usually attacked by red spider but a preventative spray with insecticide 2 or 3 times a year will keep them pest-free.

51

Lobivia

This genus of cacti comes from Bolivia (its name is an anagram of the country) but is also found in Argentina and Peru. It is outstanding for its large, freely produced flowers which come in a variety of colours from white through every shade of yellow, orange, pink, red and purple. *Lobivia maximiliana* (p.53) has bicoloured red and yellow flowers. They vary in appearance but are mostly globular plants, offsetting after 3–4 years to form clumps 6–8in (15–20cm) or more, with spines usually coloured brown or blackish. They are not at all difficult to grow and will usually flower if kept in a sunny place. Generally the more sun they receive the more flowers they will produce, although each bloom lasts only a day or two.

Lobivia jajoiana is one of the few species commonly seen which tends to stay solitary for some time and the only one with hooked spines. The flowers are brightly coloured and the black ring in the centre contrasts strikingly with the petals and with the creamy anthers which fill the cup of the flower.

Light: For maximum flower production keep on a sunny windowsill or in a greenhouse, where shading is unnecessary unless temperatures rise above 100°F (38°C). In poor light they soon grow out of shape and do not produce healthy new spines — or flowers.

Lobivia rebutioides var *chlorogana* is one of a complex group which are liable to nearly smother themselves with flowers. The blooms last barely a day or two but will come each year if the plant is potted on regularly into the next size of container and kept growing well.

Temperature: Keep above 40°F (4°C) in winter and below 100°F (38°C) in summer, giving them fresh air when possible.
Water: Water weekly in spring and summer, or fortnightly for plants in pots of 5in (13cm) or more. Always check soil has dried out from previous watering. Tail off watering in autumn to once every 3 weeks to a month, and keep dry in winter.
Feeding: Use a high potash fertilizer (as used for tomatoes) monthly in spring and summer.
Soil: Use 1 part coarse, gritty sand (not builders' or seashore) to 2 parts soil-less or good loam-based potting compost, No. 2 for small plants, No. 3 for large.
Repotting: In the early years these plants

hould be repotted every year into slightly larger pots in spring, until they reach 5in (13cm) pots, when every other year will do. At this size they can be repotted into the same size pot. Shake off the old compost carefully and replace with new. Do not water for a fortnight after repotting.

Cleaning and pest control: Spray if dusty and incorporate an insecticide 2 or 3 times a year to combat pests.

Other species: The selection is considerable and the variation of types as wide as can be, from those with very few strong spines to those which are completely obscured by a dense spiny covering. Some have single heads which never grow more than 4in (10cm) tall, yet others grow in clumps up to 12in (30cm) or more across. Most flower easily and a good selection is as follows: *L. maximiliana* (below); *L. jajoiana*, with flowers varying from yellow, through orange to red, with a black throat; *L. rebutioides*, with yellow flowers; *L. backebergiana*, with carmine flowers which have a blue sheen to the petals; *L. winterana*, with long-tubed deep pink flowers; and *L. hastifera*, with pale pink flowers, white in the throat.

Removing dead flowers

It is advisable to remove dead flowers before autumn and winter. If left on the plant they may encourage rotting from the point of attachment or harbour mealy bugs.

If mealy bugs attack, remove wool with small paintbrush dipped in methylated spirits and spray plant with diluted malathion. Repeat in 10 days if not clear.

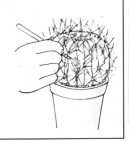

Lobivia maximiliana produces its striking red and yellow flowers in summer when it is 2in (5cm) across and 3–4 years old. They grow from the sides of the plant, beginning as small, furry buds. Once open they last for only a day or two.
L. maximiliana grows eventually to about 2½–3½in (6–8cm) tall and 1½–2in (4–5cm) wide.

Mammillaria

Mammillarias come mainly from Mexico, where they grow in habitats which range from steep rock faces and ledges in the high mountains to sandy, flat areas within salt-spray distance of the sea. Over 200 species are known, varying from single acorn-sized plants to massive clumps that would fill a wheelbarrow. The flowers are every shade between white, yellow, pink, red and purple, produced freely by most species, growing in rings around the crown of the stems. Spines are arranged in geometric whorls and may be strong and sharp, like tentmakers' needles, or as thin and flexible as hairs; straight, curved, twisting or hooked like fish-hooks; sparse or so dense as to hide the plant's body completely; coloured from black through reds, browns and yellows to pure white, often supplemented by thick wool which gives a complete covering.

If repotted and fed regularly, *Mammillaria compressa* will form a clump 12in (30cm) or more across in about 10 years growing. The plant here is in a 15in (38cm) pan and is at least 15 years old.

Light: A sunny position, particularly in winter and spring when buds are formed.
Temperature: All but one or two species will be happy with a minimum winter temperature of 40°F (4°C), but 45°F (7°C) is safer; keep below 100°F (38°C) in summer and give fresh air whenever possible.
Water: Weekly in spring and summer, fortnightly for pots of 5in (13cm) or more. Monthly in autumn and keep dry in winter.
Feeding: Feed monthly in spring and summer with high potash fertilizer (as used for tomatoes).
Soil: Use 1 part coarse gritty sand (not builders' or seashore) to 2 parts soil-less or good loam-based No. 2 compost.
Repotting: Repot every year until plant fills 5in (13cm) pot, then every other year is sufficient unless plants outgrow their container. Use half-pots or pans except for species with thick tuberous roots.

Mammillaria candida is named for its dense covering of white spines. The shell-pink flowers appear after the plant has grown to about 3in (8cm) wide and tall, perhaps sooner if plenty of sunlight is available.

Cleaning and pest control: Spray once a month to keep dust-free and incorporate an insecticide 2 or 3 times a year to combat pests.

Other species: *Mammillaria zeilmanniana* (below), with its purple flowers is one of the most popular. It is impossible to list all the species available here and the following is only a selection of some of the most attractive and rewarding plants: *M. blossfeldiana*, hooked spines, carmine striped flowers; *M. bocasana*, white, hairy spines, cream or pink flowers; *M. candida*, white or pinkish spines, pale pink flowers; *M. carmenae*, dense yellow spines, white flowers; *M. compressa*, long white spines, deep pink flowers; *M. erythrosperma*, hooked spines, dusky pink flowers; *M. hahniana*, long white hairs, purplish-red flowers; *M. longiflora*, hooked spines, large pink flowers; *M. guelzowiana*, long hairs, hooked spines, large pink flowers, over 2in (5–6cm) across; *M. microhelia*, star-like spines, greenish or pink flowers; *M. prolifera*, clustering, yellow or brown spines, yellow flowers; *M. saboae*, tiny heads and spines, large pink flowers; *M. schiedeana*, soft golden spines, white flowers; *M. schwarzii*, dense white spines, cream flowers.

Mammillaria zeilmanniana flowers in spring and summer when it has reached about 1–1½in (3–4cm) tall. Flowers appear over a period of a month or so, each lasting for around a week. Offsets, producing their own flowers, cluster around its base when it is 2–3 years old and can be used for propagation. The plant grows to 2–2½in (5–6cm) tall, 1–1½in (3–4cm) wide in a pot.

Offsets

1. Remove offsets from around the base with a clean, sharp knife, cutting at narrowest point. Do not do this while plant is flowering. Offsets should be at least ½in (1cm) across.

2. Dust base with hormone rooting powder containing fungicide and leave to dry for at least 2 days. Then plant in fresh compost. Keep in a light place but do not water for 2–3 weeks, when roots will have developed.

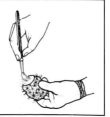

Neochilenia

These cacti, from Chile, produce flowers of delicate pastel shades, unlike the bright colours of most cacti. They are usually low-growing, small, globular plants, with darkly pigmented bodies and black, brown or yellow spines. They rarely grow more than 3in (7cm) tall and do not produce offsets. *Neochilenia nigriscoparia* (p.57) is a good example of the genus.

The funnel-shaped flowers, about 1½ to 2in (3–5cm) wide, grow from the centre of the plant and come in shades of white, cream, yellow or pink. They are sometimes spicily scented.

Some botanists maintain that the name Neochilenia is incorrect and that they should either be called Nichelia or be merged into the genus Neoporteria (p.58). Few collectors and no nurseries follow their guidance and most collectors cling to the name Neochilenia for these clearly differentiated plants.

Light: Keep on a sunny windowsill, or in a greenhouse, where they should be kept shaded in the hottest months.
Temperature: Keep above 40°F (4°C) in winter, and below 100°F (38°C) in summer, giving fresh air whenever possible.
Water: Water once a month in spring, increasing in summer to once a fortnight. In hot weather, if soil dries out quickly, water once a week. Keep dry in winter. Overwatering will rot roots and may kill the plant.
Feeding: Feed once a month in spring and summer with high potash fertilizer (as used for tomatoes).
Soil: Use 2 parts soil-less or good loam-based No. 2 potting compost with 1 part coarse, gritty sand (not builders' or seashore).

Neochilenia imitans is one of the few Neochilenias which eventually grow into columns and has tiny, close-pressed spines in neat rows. The buds are almost black and the pale yellow interior of the flower when it opens comes as a surprise. It is a slow growing species, taking 5 years to reach 2in (5cm) tall.

Neochilenia kesselringianus with its flat-globular growth and dark spines is typical of the genus. The flowers, their dark throats contrasting well with pale pink petals, are spicily scented. It rarely grows to more than about 3in (8cm) wide but will flower when 3 years old and only half this size.

Repotting: Repot every year until plants fill 4in (10cm) pot, then repot every other year or replace in same sized container with fresh soil. Be careful not to damage the thick roots when repotting and choose a pot large enough to accommodate them comfortably, with room for fresh soil round them.

Cleaning and pest control: Spray monthly to keep dust-free and incorporate an insecticide 2 or 3 times a year.

Other species: Seed is produced commercially for many of the 50 or 60 species and different species consequently appear from time to time. A good selection in addition to *N. nigriscoparia* (below) is: *N. napina*, with short black spines and cream flowers, and its variety *spinosior*, with long black spines and pink flowers; *N. imitans*, with tiny spines and pale yellow flowers; *N. jussieui*, with strong brownish spines and pink flowers with darker midstripe; *N. chilensis*, one of the most densely spined, has yellow or white spines and pink-red flowers; *N. kesselringianus* with white flowers and a neat arrangement of areoles. *N. atra*, a low-growing cactus with a very dark body and pale yellow flowers with blackish outer petals, is attractive but seldom available.

Sciara fly
If plant not growing and black flies are around soil, examine roots for sciara fly larvae. If roots are damaged, pare away soft tissue until firm healthy root remains. Dust with rooting powder.

Neochilenia nigriscoparia has a naturally dark body with long black spines. It produces fresh spines in spring and summer and after it is about 2in (5cm) wide, at 4–5 years old, funnel–shaped flowers appear from its centre in early summer. The flush of blooms lasts for about a week and it will not normally flower again until the following year.

Neoporteria

The genus of Neoporteria is sometimes considered to include Neochilenias (p.56) but as the two groups of cacti look very different, most collectors prefer to give them separate names.

Neoporteria multicolor (p.59) is typical of the group usually known as Neoporterias. These are densely spiny plants with little of the plant visible through the basketwork of interlacing, curving spines. They grow quite large, to 8in (20cm) or more tall and 4–5in (10–12cm) wide after 10 or 12 years and usually remain single headed. The spines vary in colour from creamy white through yellows and browns to black, and are mostly long, curving inwards to make an almost impenetrable, porcupine-like covering where they meet at the top of the plant. Almost but not quite impenetrable, for this is where the flowers push their way through.

Neoporteria flowers are unlike almost any other cactus flowers in shape, the outer petals curving out, the inner staying close around the centre parts of the flower. They are usually bicoloured in varying shades of pink and yellow.

Neoporteria wagenknechtii has strong, needle-sharp spine which make repotting difficult. It flowers at about 2in (5cm) wide and tall, when it is about 4 or 5 years old. This plant has buds, open flowers and the yellow remains of dead flowers.

Light: Give maximum sunshine on a sunny windowsill or in a greenhouse all year round.

Temperature: Keep above 40°F (4°C) in winter and below 100°F (38°C) in summer, giving fresh air whenever possible.

Water: Water fortnightly in summer, weekly if in pots smaller than 4in (10cm) as long as compost has dried out between waterings. In spring and autumn water monthly and keep dry in winter.

Feeding: Use a high potash fertilizer (as used for tomatoes) once a month during spring and summer.

Soil: Use 2 parts coarse gritty sand (not builders' or seashore) to 3 parts soil-less or good loam-based No. 2 potting compost.

Repotting: Repot every year until plant fills a 5in (13cm) pot, then every other year. If plant has not outgrown its container, remove it from pot, shake off the old soil and repot in same pot with fresh soil. Do not rewater for 2 weeks. Take care when repotting as the spines are very sharp.

Cleaning and pest control: Spray monthly to keep dust-free and incorporate an insecticide 2 or 3 times a year to combat pests.

Other species: Several different species are often available as seed is produced commercially and the cacti are not difficult to grow. Three good ones in addition to N. *multicolor* (right) are: N. *laniceps*, with fine, almost hair-like khaki-brown to dark brown spines; N. *litoralis*, usually with yellow spines; and N. *wagenknechtii* with strong spines and pink flowers.

Repotting

Wear gloves to protect your hands and handle plant with care to avoid damaging the sharp spines.

1. Remove plant from old pot and examine root ball. If there are plenty of hair-like white roots on surface, it needs repotting. Check for signs of pests. For treatment see pp 12–15.

2. Gently crumble root ball with fingers to remove old compost but be careful not to break roots. If compost falls away easily and there are plenty of new roots, plant may be repotted in same pot with fresh compost.

3. If root ball is solid, prepare pot 1 size larger with drainage material and 1in (2½cm) layer of fresh compost. Place root ball on compost.

4. Trickle fresh compost around root ball, firm down gently and add final top layer of grit. Compost level should be the same as before, about 1in (2½cm) below pot rim. Do not water for 2 weeks, to allow roots to grow into new compost.

Neoporteria multicolor has pines which range in colour rom almost white to nearly lack, with every shade of ellow and brown between.

If given enough sunlight, it will flower in late summer when it is about 3in (7cm) wide, at 5–6 years old.

Between 12 and 15 flowers appear over a period of about 2 weeks and have the characteristic Neoporteria

shape with outer petals curving outwards and inner ones remaining almost closed around the flower's centre.

Notocactus

The name Notocactus means 'southerly cactus' and refers to the plant's origins in South America where it grows in Argentina, Uruguay, Paraguay and Brazil. These are among the largest flowered of the cacti, usually with yellow, silky-textured blooms up to 5in (12cm) across. The flowers are freely produced once the plants are about 3in (7–8cm) wide after 4–5 years and steadily increase in size and number as the plant gets larger. Most are easy to grow and many have decorative spines as well as sumptuous flowers. *Notocactus leninghausii* (p.61), sometimes called the Teddybear cactus, is probably the best known.

Light: Keep on a sunny windowsill for best flowering. If in a greenhouse, shade lightly in summer.

Temperature: Keep above 45°F (8°C) in winter and below 100°F (38°C) in summer. Give fresh air whenever possible.

Water: Unlike most cacti, these should not be allowed to dry out completely in winter, provided the temperature is at least 45°F (8°C). Water monthly from base of pot. In spring, increase watering to once a fortnight and in summer weekly watering may be necessary if soil is drying out quickly. Reduce watering again in autumn.

Feeding: Feed monthly in spring and summer with high potash fertilizer (as used for tomatoes).

Soil: 3 parts soil-less or good loam-based No. 2 potting compost, with 1 part coarse, gritty sand (not builders' or seashore).

Repotting: Repot every year in next size pot until plants fill a 5in (13cm) pot. Then every other year will be sufficient. Some Notocactus species grow more quickly than others, so check whether plant is outgrowing its pot. There should be room for fresh soil to be added around the plant when the old has been shaken off the roots.

Notocactus crassigibbus produces large flowers which, in full sun, will flatten out and cover the plant body completely. It starts to flower when 2 or 3in (5–8cm) wide, at 4 or 5 years old. This plant is in a 5in (14cm) pot.

Notocactus purpureus is one of a group which tends to produce its flowers in later summer, when most cacti, including other Notocacti, have finished. Generally staying solitary, this species will flower at about 2 or 3in (5–8cm) wide, when it is about 4 or 5 years old.

Cleaning and pest control: Spray monthly to keep dust-free and use an insecticide 2 or 3 times a year to combat pests.

Other species: Among those with a dense covering of spines are *N. scopa*, with red and white spines and smallish yellow flowers, *N. haselbergii*, with white spines and red flowers, *N. graessneri*, with yellow spines and small green flowers, and the superb, blue-bodied, soft yellow spined *N. magnificus*. This is much larger than most others and has large yellow flowers.

Individual heads grow to the size of a large melon, forming clusters which fill a 10in (25cm) pan. These densely spined species are sometimes known as Eriocactus or Brasilicactus. Others worth looking out for are *N. crassigibbus*, with 5in (12cm) yellow flowers, *N. buiningii*, with milky-green bodies and yellow flowers, *N. horstii*, orange flowers, *N. uebelmannianus*, purple flowers, *N. rutilans*, pink flowers, *N. ottonis*, with yellow flowers and *N. purpureus* with purplish-pink flowers.

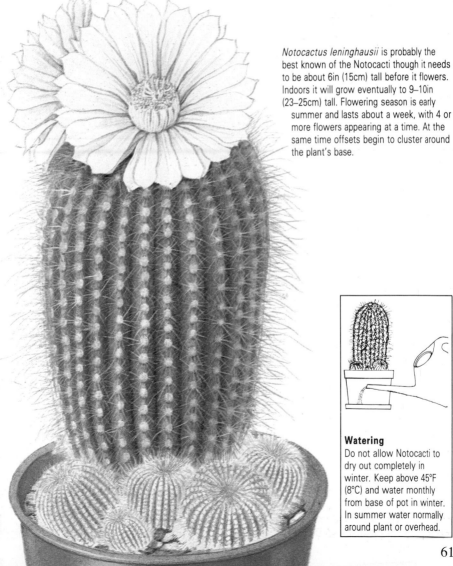

Notocactus leninghausii is probably the best known of the Notocacti though it needs to be about 6in (15cm) tall before it flowers. Indoors it will grow eventually to 9–10in (23–25cm) tall. Flowering season is early summer and lasts about a week, with 4 or more flowers appearing at a time. At the same time offsets begin to cluster around the plant's base.

Watering
Do not allow Notocacti to dry out completely in winter. Keep above 45°F (8°C) and water monthly from base of pot in winter. In summer water normally around plant or overhead.

Opuntia

This is the largest genus of cacti, spreading from as far south as Argentina through the Americas to Canada. It has been introduced and naturalized in many other parts of the world, particularly in the Mediterranean — and grows so freely in Australia that it has become a problem. Most Opuntias have flat, disc-shaped segments but there are small, round-jointed species and others with cylindrical segments. They range in size from a few inches to several feet. Most are easy to grow indoors though some of the larger types need more room than most people can provide. However, only a few produce flowers unless they are in a very sunny position all the year round. *Opuntia albata* (p.63) with its attractive yellow flowers, is one of the easier ones and blooms when it is 3–4 years old.

Opuntia oligotricha is one of a group of papery-spined cylindrical-jointed species with segments that are easily knocked off. In the right position they will flower when they are about 6in (15cm) tall, at about 3 or 4 years old but will not do so unless they have plenty of sunshine all the year round.

Light: Maximum sunlight on a sunny windowsill is needed for strong growth. If the light is not ideal, they will soon grow out of shape and need to be supported. Full sun at all times of the year is needed for flowers.

Temperature: Keep above 40°F (4°C) in winter and below 100°F (38°C) in summer. Give fresh air whenever possible.

Water: Water once a week in summer, providing soil dries out between waterings, fortnightly in spring and autumn. Keep dry in winter.

Feeding: Use high potash fertilizer (as used for tomatoes) once a month in spring and summer.

Soil: Use 2 parts soil-less or good loam-based No. 2 potting compost, with 1 part coarse gritty sand (not builders' or seashore).

Repotting: Repot every year until plant fills a 5in (13cm) pot. Then every other year will do. To avoid touching the sharp spines, ease

Opuntia albata grows to 5–6in (13–15cm) tall but flowers after 3 or 4 years, when it is only 2½–3in (6–8cm). Flowering season is early summer and lasts for about a week. Each flowering pad produces 3–4 pale yellow flowers from its ti. A healthy *Opuntia* will produce new segments each year and, if in good light, should not need support.

A layer of grit on top of the compost helps to prevent the soil becoming hard and compacted after watering, stops the lower stem being splashed with mud and retains moisture in the pot in hot weather.

plant out of the pot until you can grasp
e root-ball. For large plants, you will need
lp.

eaning and pest control: Spray monthly to
ep dust-free and incorporate an
secticide 2 or 3 times a year to combat
sts. Make sure both sides of the stems are
rayed.

ther species: Few of the cylindrical jointed
ecies are grown indoors since they rarely
oduce the wonderful spines they have in
e wild but *O. tunicata* is sometimes
ailable. This has glistening, creamy-white
ines and loosely attached joints. Another
nich sometimes flowers is *O. oligotricha*.
f the low-growing small-jointed species
ere are many. *O. invicta* has marvellously
ood-red new spines but is slow-growing,
king 5 years or more to fill a 7in (18cm) pot
pan. *O. molinensis* has dense ginger tufts
spines and *O. nigrispina* is purplish-black.

Taking cuttings
1. After flowering has
finished, cut whole segment
from plant at narrowest
point with a sharp knife.

2. Dust end of cutting and
cut end of stem with
hormone rooting powder
containing fungicide. Leave
cutting to dry for at least 2
days.

3. Prepare 2 or 3in (5 or
8cm) pot with potting
compost and place cutting
on surface, bottom end
against compost.

4. Cover just enough to
hold it upright or rest against
side of pot. Keep in good
light place (not sunny) for
2–3 weeks until roots
develop. Then start watering.
Repot when roots fill pot.

Opuntias kept in poor light
soon lose their round, disc
shape and grow elongated
and pale greenish-yellow. Cut
off elongated stems and
reposition plant in better
light, moving gradually over a
few weeks into a sunny
position.

Opuntia albata has spines
with no barbs and others of
this type (but with barbs)
worth growing are
O.microdasys with yellow,
red-brown or white spines;
O. basilaris,with purplish-
violet pads and *O. violacea*
var. *santa-rita*, with long
spines and violet pads. All
these can be grown until
they fill a 7in (18cm) pot but
when larger than this, it is
best to root one of the pads
and start a new plant.

Parodia

Since they were introduced to cultivation some forty years ago, these cacti
have become very popular with
collectors because of their attractive
spines and freely produced flowers.
They are small plants, the largest not
more than 8 or 12in (20 or 30cm) tall,
and take ten years or more to reach this
size. Since they have shallow roots,
they do not usually outgrow a 4in
(10cm) pot. Flower colours vary from
deep red as in *Parodia penicillata* (p.65)
through orange and yellow and spines
range from pure white through yellows
and browns to almost black. They come
from a wide area of south America
including Bolivia, Paraguay and
Argentina.

Parodia comosa has neat rows of fluffy white pads called
areoles, from which the contrasting dark brown spines
arise. An abudance of smallish yellow flowers may be
expected when the plant is 4 or 5 years old and 2in (5cm)
so tall. As with all cacti that have white wool, overhead
watering or spraying should be avoided.

Light: A sunny windowsill is essential for
good spine and flower production. In a
greenhouse, shade lightly in the sunniest
months, giving full light for the rest of the
year.

Temperature: They do best about 45°F
(8°C) in winter but will survive at 40°F (4°C).
In summer keep below 100°F (38°C), giving
fresh air whenever possible.

Water: Water every week in summer, every
fortnight if in pots larger than 4in (10cm).
Reduce to once a month in spring and
autumn, keeping dry in winter in the coldest
months.

Feeding: Use high potash fertilizer (as used
for tomatoes) 2 or 3 times during spring and
summer.

Soil: Use 3 parts soil-less or good loam-
based No. 2 potting compost to 1 part coarse
gritty sand (not builders' or seashore).

Repotting: Repot every year in spring into
next size pot until plants are in 4in (10cm)
pot. Then every other year will do. If plant
has not outgrown its container, remove
from pot, carefully shake old soil from
around roots and replace with fresh soil.

Parodia husteiniana is notable for its dense, warm amber
spines, many of which are hooked and may easily catch o
curtains or clothing. If accidentally unpotted in this way,
replace in dry compost and do not water for 2 weeks. This
species flowers when it is barely an inch (2½cm) tall.

arodia penicillata grows 4–6in (10–15cm) tall and
*o*duces its clusters of red flowers in early summer.
*f*owering season may last from a week to a month with
ew blooms replacing those that fade. Though Parodias
*r*ow slowly, most reach flowering size when they are only
*b*out 1in (2½cm) across.

If growing from seed, leave
the tray or pots covered with
polythene for about a year.
After 6 months the seedlings
will still be only about the
size of pinheads, often with a
tiny root. If the covering is
removed too soon, they will
quickly dry up.

Most have shallow roots so half-pots or pans
are suitable.

Cleaning and pest control: Spray monthly to
keep dust-free except for the very woolly
species such as *P. nivosa* and *schwebsiana*.
Incorporate an insecticide 2 or 3 times a year.

Other species: *P. chrysacanthion* is similar
to *P. penicillata* (above) but has yellow
flowers produced at the centre in clusters of
10 or more. It is one of the most beautifully
spined of all cacti, with dense, long, thin
spines like fragile splinters of yellow glass.

Many smaller growing types are available in
various spines and flower colours. These
include *P. comosa* with yellow flowers and
P. hausteiniana with hooked yellow spines
and yellow flowers. *P. nivosa* is a more
woolly species with snow-white spines and
red flowers; *P. prolifera* makes clusters of
small heads with white and yellow spines
and deep yellow flowers. *P. maassii* is one of
the largest with spines ranging from white to
yellow or brown and yellow or orange
flowers.

65

Rebutia

Rebutias are among the best cacti for beginners: they grow well on a sunny windowsill and flower freely from the time they are 1in (2½cm) tall. They grow in clusters but rarely need more than a 5 or 6in (13cm) pot. Their spines are weak and flexible and flower colours range from red, orange, pink to yellow and white. *Rebutia perplexa* (p.67) is a recent introduction now widely available.

Light: A sunny windowsill or greenhouse will give best flower production.

Temperature: If kept dry they will take temperatures of below freezing, but for safety keep above 40°F (4°C) in winter. Keep below 100°F (38°C) in summer and give fresh air whenever possible.

Water: Water weekly in summer (fortnightly if in pans of 5in (13cm) or more), monthly in spring and autumn, with none at all in winter.

Feeding: Use a high potash fertilizer (as used for tomatoes) 3 or 4 times in the spring and summer.

Soil: Use 3 parts soil-less or good loam-based No. 2 potting compost with 1 part coarse, gritty sand (not builders' or seashore).

Repotting: Repot every year in next size pan or half-pot until 5in (13cm) pan is reached, when every other year will do unless plant has grown right up to or over the sides of its container. If it has not filled container, replace it in the same sized pan with new compost after shaking the old soil off the roots.

Cleaning and pest control: Spray once a month to keep dust-free and incorporate an insecticide 2 or 3 times a year to combat pests. Most Rebutias are particularly susceptible to red spider and also to mealy bug.

Other species: Without exception the 50 or more species available from cactus nurseries

Rebutia albiflora was almost unknown 20 years ago but has quickly become a favourite. Its tiny stems have glassy white, bristle-like spines and it flowers freely at only ½in (1cm) tall when it is a year or two old. It is easily propagate from the lightly attached offsets but is susceptible to red spider.

Rebutia flavistyla is a fairly recent introduction now freely available. It will produce its rich reddish-orange flowers at 2 or 3 years old, when it will be an inch or so (3cm) wide.

cluster freely and will flower easily. A good selection of the many to choose from would be: *R. perplexa*, *R. albiflora*, with tiny, acorn-sized heads, white spines and flowers; *R. marsoneri* and *R. aureiflora*, with rich deep yellow flowers; *R. krainziana*, with short, neat white spines, dark bodies and blood red flowers; *R. kupperana*, with long, bristly spines, brown and yellow, and fiery red flowers; *R. haagei*, small cone-shaped heads and salmon-pink flowers; *R. violaciflora*, with lilac-pink flowers; *R. muscula*, with dense, short white spines and orange flowers; *R. kariusiana*, with pale pink flowers and *R. flavistyla* with reddish-orange flowers.

Rebutia haagei is one of a group of Rebutias sometimes labelled Mediolobivia which make dense clusters of brownish-grey stems and produce many red or pink flowers. In this species they fade from deep to pale salmon-pink, each bloom lasting a week or more. They flower at 2 or 3 years old when they are barely 1in (2½cm) tall.

Rebutia perplexa grows as clusters of small, green heads with yellow spines. Its lovely rose-pink flowers grow from around the base after about a year's cultivation, the late spring flowering season lasting from a week to a month. A healthy plant will also produce new, brightly coloured spines at the centre of each head. Like all Rebutias it is susceptible to red spider mite and if the skin begins to turn brown all over, this is usually a sign that the pest is present.

Schlumbergera

The name Schlumbergera is now accepted as the correct one for the well-known Christmas cactus (Zygocactus) which, as its common name implies, comes into flower in Europe's mid-winter. In fact, though some flower for Christmas, for others the natural flowering season is later.

They grow wild in the jungles of Brazil so need rather different treatment from desert cacti. They need peat-based, soil-less composts, watering all the year round and slightly less light than other cacti and are generally treated more like an ordinary indoor plant. There are many different forms to choose from as breeders have produced numerous hybrids, usually with toothed stems and flower colours ranging from white through pinks and reds to purple. All have the familiar segmented stems, with flowers appearing at the ends of segments grown earlier in the year.

There are many coloured hybrid Schlumbergeras to choose from but some of the most sought after are the paler forms like this S. 'Wintermarchen'. They will flower a year or two after rooting, when they have made a few new stems.

Light: They do well on a sunny windowsill indoors but if grown in a greenhouse should be kept out of long periods of continuous sunlight: 2–3 hours a day are about right. Shade the greenhouse lightly in the hottest months.

Temperature: Keep above 40°F (4°C) in winter but a temperature of about 50°F (10°C) is better, especially for producing flowers at around Christmas time. Keep below 100°F (38°C) in summer, giving fresh air whenever possible.

Water: Water once a month in winter to prevent soil from drying out completely, fortnightly in spring and autumn. In summer water every week, allowing soil just to dry out between waterings.

Feeding: Use high potash fertilizer once a month in the spring, summer and autumn. Do not feed while flowering.

oil: Soil-less, peat-based compost is best ith no additional material. Some growers refer leafmould, which is more like their atural surroundings.

epotting: Schlumbergeras grow quickly nd may reach 12in (30cm) across in 3–4 ears. Repot each year into next size pot, andling the root ball carefully as they islike having their roots disturbed. The ase of the plant becomes woody with age nd it is a good idea to propagate new plants.

Cleaning and pest control: Spray at least once a week to keep them fresh and dust-free. Incorporate an insecticide 2 or 3 times a year to combat pests and a systemic fungicide to prevent the orange and brown spotting which sometimes affects them.

Other species: The many hybrids of the popular Christmas cactus all flower in mid-winter but a later-flowering species, known as the Easter cactus, blooms in spring and has bright red flowers.

Stem segments
A month after flowering, take cutting of 2 segments, cutting at joint with a sharp knife.

2. Dust both cut ends with hormone rooting powder containing fungicide and leave to dry for 2 days. Place end of cutting gently into almost dry soil-less compost, planting about ½in (1cm) deep. Water after 2 weeks.

These plants appreciate a weekly spray with distilled or rainwater – tap water tends to leave marks. Spray more often in warm weather, in the evenings.

Two similar plants worth looking out for are *S. (Rhipsalidopsis) rosea,* with lilac pink flowers and stem segments each only an inch (3cm) long and *S. (Epiphyllanthus) obovatus* which looks like a small-stemmed Opuntia and has scarlet flowers.

A healthy Schlumbergera will make new segments on all its stems and will flower in winter. The flowers appear at the ends of the newest segments and last for 1 or 2 weeks.

Selenicereus

This is the famous, clambering cactus known as Queen of the Night, because of its enormous, white, scented flowers which bloom for one night only. It is a vigorous grower and in the right conditions will make yards of growth each year. For best results it needs either a large pot or to be planted in a corner of a greenhouse. The stem must be looped in and out around a large trellis or cane or twined along the sides and ridge bar of a greenhouse. Old, woody growth should be cut out every year and the plant treated rather like a cultivated blackberry or climbing rose. If it is not pruned it will quickly become a tangled mess. The different species come from Cuba, Haiti, Mexico and Texas where they grow rooted in the soil and clamber among the upper branches of trees.

This plant, believed to be *Selenicereus grandiflorus*, clambers along the ridge bar of a 12ft (3½m) greenhouse where it is trained back and forth. The huge flowers, 8–12i (20–30cm) across, are produced in summer and open on warm evenings to fill the greenhouse with their perfume.

Light: Full sunlight at all times is needed, on a sunny windowsill or porch. In a greenhouse the root can be planted in a shady corner so long as the stem is trained into the lightest position possible. Without full light it will not produce its flowers.

Temperature: It will stand 40°F (4°C) in winter but is best at 45–50°F (7–10°C). Keep below 100°F (38°C) in summer and give fresh air whenever possible.

Water: In spring and summer water once a fortnight, or once a month if in a big pot 9in (23cm) or more. Allow soil to dry out between waterings. In early autumn stop watering to allow pot to dry out before temperatures fall too much, then keep dry in winter.

Feeding: Feed monthly in spring and summer with high potash fertilizer (as used for tomatoes).

Soil: Use soil-less or good loam-based No. 2 potting compost with no added grit or sand.

Repotting: Repot every year in spring until roots fill a 9in (23cm) pot. Then change soil every 3 years, replacing plant in same sized pot unless roots have outgrown it. Cut old wood when repotting. In years plant is not repotted, cut out old wood in spring, if stems are tangled and unsightly.

Cleaning and pest control: Spray weekly with water in spring and summer, incorporating an insecticide 2 or 3 times a year to combat pests.

Other species: There are half-a-dozen or so names but it is difficult to be sure of the accuracy of any in cultivation. All look similar and all produce the large flowers for which they are famous. Named species sometimes found are *S. grandiflorus*, *S. macdonaldiae* and *S. pseudospinulosus*.

Training

1. Start training when plant is 3ft (1m) long. First repot into large pot with room for root ball and space around for growth.

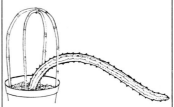

2. Insert 2 pliable canes (as used for basket-making) at opposite sides of pot, pushing them well down. Tie them firmly at top where they cross.

3. As stem lengthens, weave it around the canes. It is important to train while still young and flexible as older stems become woody.

Selenicereus pteranthus should flower after 3–5 years, when its stems are 2–3ft (60–90cm) long. The flowers, about 10in (25cm) across, appear 2 or 3 at a time in the summer, the flowering season lasting about a month. The flowers open in the evening, bloom for the night and by morning are finished.

Sulcorebutia

Ten years ago only a handful of Sulcorebutias were known and they were rare in cultivation. Now there are some 40 or 50 to choose from and they are becoming increasingly popular with collectors since they are extremely free flowering. They come originally from the mountains of Bolivia where they grow at about 9,000ft (about 3000m) and were at first grouped with Rebutia species (p.66) but are now considered to be a separate genus.

Sulcorebutias grow only slowly, taking 8 to 10 years to fill a 6–8in (15–20cm) pan but they flower when they are less than an inch across, often when they are only 2 years old. Flower and spine colours vary: *Sulcorebutia rauschii* (p.75) with its bright, electric pink flowers, is perhaps the best looking of them all.

Sulcorebutia glomeriseta has an absolutely impenetrable covering of fine, bristly spines. The many, rich yellow flower are produced sporadically throughout the summer when it 2 or 3 years old and an inch (2½cm) wide.

Light: As mountain cacti they are used to very bright light so they need the sunniest possible windowsill to ensure compact growth and good flowers. Do not shade in the greenhouse.

Temperature: They will survive below freezing temperatures in an unheated greenhouse but must be kept quite dry. In summer keep below 100°F (38°C) and give fresh air whenever possible.

Water: Keep dry in winter and water once a month in spring and autumn. In summer, water weekly (fortnightly if in 5in (13cm) pots or more), making sure soil dries out between waterings.

Feeding: Feed 3 or 4 times in spring and summer with high potash fertilizer (as used for tomatoes).

Soil: Use 2 parts soil-less or good loam-based No. 2 potting compost to 1 part coarse gritty sand (not builders' or seashore).

Repotting: Repot every year until in a 5in (13cm) pot, then every other year will be

Sulcorebutia canigueralii is a popular, easily grown specie with short spines and purple-brown or green stems. The bicoloured flowers are freely produced at 2 or 3 years old, when the plant is only about an inch (2½cm) tall.

nough. If roots do not fill pot, repot in ame sized container with fresh soil.

Cleaning and pest control: Spray monthly with water to keep dust-free and incorporate an insecticide 2 or 3 times a year o combat pests.

Other species: A good selection of the many now available is: *S. alba*, with white spines and pink or red flowers; *S. canigueralii*, with brown spines and two-coloured flowers, red with a yellow throat; *S. arenacea*, with wonderfully neat, short, white spines and yellow flowers; *S. candiae*, with yellow pines and flowers; *S. flavissima*, with bright yellow spines, pink flowers; *S. lepida* with dark brown spines and deep purple-red flowers; *S. glomeriseta*, with flexible, bristly spines and yellow flowers; *S. pulchra*, with deep red flowers; *S. mizquensis*, with short white spines and lilac flowers; and *S. rauschii* (below).

Repotting

1. Loosen pot from around root ball by squeezing it gently on one side, then the other, then ease root ball out sideways into gloved hand. Try to grasp root ball not plant.

2. If loose soil is around root, crumble it gently, being careful not to damage roots. If no loose soil, do not try to loosen it.

3. Prepare clean pot 1 size larger and add 1–2in (2½–5cm) fresh soil. Place plant on soil and trickle new soil around roots. Firm gently around plant. Do not water for 2 weeks.

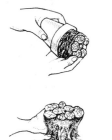

Sulcorebutia rauschii flowers when it is only about ½in (1cm) tall, after 2 years growth. The flowers appear in spring or summer, the season lasting for a month or more. Heads grow to about 1½in (4cm) wide and form clumps of offsets which will eventually fill a 6in (15cm) pot. *S. rauschii* comes in several different forms, with purple or green bodies and black or golden spines. All have the striking electric pink flowers.

Thelocactus

This small genus of desert cacti comes from the very dry areas of Texas and Mexico. Most are solitary plants though some will produce offsets in cultivation after five or six years. They may be flat, squat or pyramid-shaped and many grow on a turnip-like root which needs room to develop in a deep pot. Spines may be long and curving, or straight and thick and may form either a dense covering or a sparser pattern on the tubercles. Flowers usually range from white through red to violet. *Thelocactus bicolor* (p.77), the most popular species and probably the easiest, has pink and red flowers and attractive red and yellow spines. These are not the easiest cacti to grow as they are susceptible to overwatering but if you follow instructions carefully, they will grow and produce their attractive flowers when they are only about 2in (5cm) across.

Thelocactus bicolor var. *bolansis,* from Mexico, is a more columnar, very densely spined variety, with the body almost obscured by a basketwork of pale yellow spines. The flowers too, are different – lilac with a white throat. It is a slower growing plant than *T. bicolor* but should flower at about 2in (5cm) tall and 4 or 5 years old.

Light: As desert cacti used to full sunshine, they need the sunniest possible position, on a sunny windowsill or in an unshaded greenhouse.

Temperature: Keep above 40°F (4°C) in winter and below 100°F (38°C) in summer, giving fresh air whenever possible.

Water: It is very important not to overwater these cacti as too much moisture will rot their thick root. Keep quite dry in winter and water only once a month in spring. In summer increase frequency to fortnightly or weekly for pots less than 3in (8cm) which dry out more quickly. Always allow soil to dry out between waterings in summer.

Feeding: Feed with high potash fertilizer (as used for tomatoes) once a month in spring and summer.

Soil: Use 2 parts soil-less or good loam-based No. 2 potting compost and 1 part coarse, gritty sand (not builders' or seashore).

Thelocactus phymatothelos is one of the low-growing types with short spines and prominent, bluish–grey tubercles. The satin-like, pale pinkish-white flowers are produced after 3 or 4 years, when the plant is 1½–2in (4–5cm) wide.

Repotting: Repot every year until plant reaches 5in (13cm) pot size, then every other year. Be careful not to damage the turnip-like root and put it in a pot deep enough to contain it. Leave dry for a fortnight after repotting.

Cleaning and pest control: Spray with water to keep dust-free 2 or 3 times a year and incorporate an insecticide to combat pests.

Other species: Two varieties of *T. bicolor* are worth looking out for. These are *T. bicolor* var. *bolansis*, with straw yellow spines and lilac flowers, and *T. bicolor* var. *flavidispinus*, with yellow and red spines and violet to lilac flowers. Two of the flatter-growing type, with very large tubercles, are *T. phymatothelos* and *T. hexaedrophorus*. These have an overall blue-grey colouring and white to pale pink flowers. Two densely spined species, both with purplish-violet flowers, are *T. conothelos*, with white and brown spines, and *T. macdowellii* (sometimes labelled *Echinomastus macdowellii*). Finally there are a few larger flat-growing species with long, curving spines: *T. nidulans*, *T. rinconensis* and *T. lophothele*, all with white to palish pink flowers.

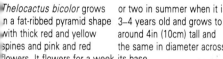

Thelocactus bicolor grows in a fat-ribbed pyramid shape with thick red and yellow spines and pink and red flowers. It flowers for a week or two in summer when it is 3–4 years old and grows to around 4in (10cm) tall and the same in diameter across its base.

Handling spiny plants
When repotting, take care not to damage spines or your hands. Wear gloves and ease plant out of pot sideways onto a padded bench, grasping the root ball not the plant body. Have the new pot ready with fresh compost in the bottom.

Uebelmannia

This is a recently discovered genus and, though it is difficult to grow on its own roots indoors, it has become quickly popular. When grown naturally it is susceptible to overwatering and possibly to low temperatures and grows very slowly — only about ½in (1cm) a year. It is usually found grafted onto a different kind of cactus and when grown like this presents few problems. It grows to the size of a grapefruit in about 5 years and occasionally even produces offsets. Uebelmannias are grown essentially for the beauty of their form, colouring and spines since flowers rarely appear on cultivated plants and when they do are small and yellow, growing in the top centre of the plant. *Uebelmannia pectinifera* (p.79) is by far the most popular species available.

Uebelmannia pseudopectinifera may in fact be a variety of the similar *U. pectinifera* (right). It differs in being olive green and less spiny than the other plant but, like it, rarely flowers in cultivation.

Light: A sunny windowsill or greenhouse is essential for good colour and compact growth.

Temperature: It is thought that winter minimum should be 50°F (10°C) but they will usually stand 45°F (7°C) without harm. Keep below 100°F (38°C) in summer and give fresh air whenever possible.

Uebelmannia buiningii is a much smaller growing plant with the rich purple body colouring of *U. pectinifera* but with fewer, wispy yellow spines and fewer ribs. The plant here is on a graft and is about 1½in (4cm) wide.

Water: If plant is growing on its own roots, water only once a fortnight in summer, monthly in spring and autumn. Keep dry in winter. If on a graft, water every week in summer and fortnightly in spring and autumn. But keep dry in winter.

Feeding: Use high potash fertilizer (as used for tomatoes) once a month in spring and summer.

Soil: Use soil-less or good loam-based No. 2 potting compost mixed with coarse gritty sand (not builders' or seashore). If on a graft use 2 parts compost to 1 part sand; if on its own roots use half and half.

Repotting: Repot every year, being careful

ot to disturb roots if plant is not grafted. If
t has not outgrown its pot, shake old soil off
oots and replace,in same container. When a
in (13cm) pot is reached, repot every other
ear.

Cleaning and pest control: Spray monthly to
keep dust-free, incorporating an insecticide
2 or 3 times a year to combat pests.

Other species: *U. pectinifera* is by far the
most common but others sometimes offered
are *U. gummifera, U. meninensis, U.
flavispina, U. buinigii* and *U. pseudopectinifera.* All are very similar in
appearance and growth habit.

Uebelmannia pectinifera is
a handsome, dark purple to
black skinned cactus with
neat rows of spines down its
ribs. It grows slowly to about
3–4in (7–10cm) tall and across
but if it is not grafted will
rarely increase more than
½in (1cm) in a year. The
yellow flowers are rare
indoors but come in summer
from the centre of the plant
when it is fully grown.

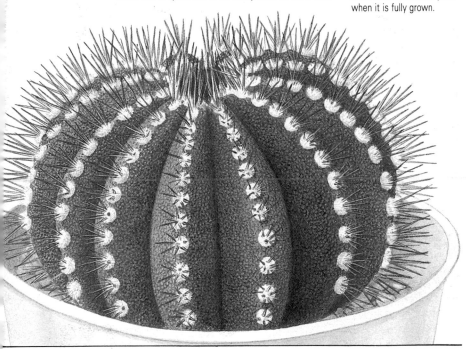

Grafting
1. Remove top inch (2½cm)
of a tall type of cactus and
cut a slice from the bottom
of the Uebelmannia with a
sharp, clean knife.

2. Immediately place the
Ucbelmannia's cut surface.
firmly on the other stump,
making sure the rings near
the centre of the stems
overlap.

3. Hold firmly in place with
elastic bands until new
growth appears. Do not
damage outer tissue with
too tight or too narrow a
band.

4. To improve appearance
of plant on graft, use deep
pot and bury rootstock in
gravel below pot rim so
that only the Uebelmannia
is visible.

Buying your cactus

Cacti can often be bought in garden centres, general nurseries and florists and sometimes they are of good quality and well cared for. More often, unfortunately, they are of poor quality, or have been wrongly cared for and are a dusty, unshining motley collection.

Remember, too, that most general nurserymen or shopkeepers have only superficial knowledge of how to care for these plants, and their advice, however well-meaning, may not be very useful.

Specialist nurseries are best for unusual cacti, and they can normally be bought either by personal visit, or, perhaps more conveniently, by post, as they travel well. The largest suppliers are not always the best and a small grower is often a better prospect, being more concerned to give you good quality and good advice, so that you come back for more. The advertisements carried by gardening journals, particularly those of the cactus societies, will lead you to the best sources. It is important before buying to consider the conditions you can provide for these plants. If you are a beginner, choose plants that are simple to grow. Do not be tempted to buy the more difficult ones to cultivate until you have gained some experience. And do not buy too many from the same source, especially by post, until you have made sure the quality is good.

Look carefully at plants you intend to buy. They should be firm in the pot, not rocking about, as this may well indicate they have already lost their roots. The plant body should be a healthy bright green, not too pale or yellowish (although some cacti have naturally purple or brown bodies these are the exception rather than the rule). The spines should be clean and brightly coloured. Generally it is safer to buy small plants and grow them on, than to pay a good deal of money for large plants, until you have gained the experience to look after them well. Do not buy plants from a situation where they may have been subject to frost.

Lastly make sure your plant has a label, so that you can look up its care instructions.

When you get it home, inspect it for pests (the roots as well), repot it into your own compost, and leave dry for 2 weeks. If possible keep it away from your other plants until you have ascertained that it is pest free. Do the same with plants sent by post. These usually arrive without pots, so get some ready in advance for their arrival.

Scientific names

Few cacti have popular names and these vary from place to place. The ones here are all identified under their full scientific names. All plants (and animals) are classified into groups known as families which are subdivided into genera (singular genus) and then again into species and varieties. Plants in the same genus but of different species share some basic characteristics but may look very different in size, shape or colouring. A variety is only slightly different from another variety of the same species. Hybrids are crosses between 2 different species or sometimes even genera. Correctly labelled plants have a genus name followed by the species and, if appropriate, the variety. For hybrids the second part of the name is put in inverted commas and is usually more popular than scientific, e.g. Chamaelobivia 'Shot Scarlet'.

The Cactus and Succulent Society of America can be contacted at 2631 Fairgreen Avenue, Arcadia, California 91006

Acknowledgements

Colour artwork by Josephine Martin and Bob Bampton/The Garden Studio
Line artwork by Patricia Newton and Marion Neville
Photography by Bill Weightman
Designed by Marion Neville